FORESTS ON FIRE

FORESTS
ON FIRE

THE FIGHT TO
SAVE OUR TREES

GREGORY VOGT

An Impact Book
Franklin Watts
New York/London/Toronto/Sydney
1990

Photographs courtesy of: National Park Service: pp. 8, 14
(T. & N. Ramhorst); Gamma-Liaison: p. 11 (Bill Saltaz);
U.S. Forest Service Collection, National Agricultural Library:
pp. 17, 20, 43, 47, 60, 66, 73, 100; AP/Wide World:
pp. 24, 34, 50, 63, 79, 110; UPI/Bettmann Newsphotos: p. 65.

Library of Congress Cataloging-in-Publication Data

Vogt, Gregory.
Forests on fire : the fight to save our trees / Gregory
Vogt.
p.   cm.—(An Impact book)
Includes bibliographical references.
Summary: Examines the devastating effects of forest fires and the
various techniques used to combat and prevent them.
ISBN 0-531-10940-2
1. Forest fires—Yellowstone National Park—Juvenile literature.
2. Forest fires—Government policy—Yellowstone National Park—
Juvenile literature.   3. Fire ecology—Yellowstone National Park—
Juvenile literature.   4. Forest fires—United States—Prevention
and control—Juvenile literature.   5. Fire ecology—United States—
Juvenile literature.   6. Yellowstone National Park—Juvenile
literature. [1. Forest fires.   2. Fire ecology.   3. Ecology.]
I. Title.
SD421.32.Y45V643   1990
634.9'618'0973—dc20   90-33662 CIP AC

CONTENTS

Wildfire is one of the most
dramatic spectacles of nature.
It is appropriate, then, to remember
two people who have made
theater a large part of their lives.
With love, friendship, and many
happy memories I dedicate
this book to my aunt and uncle
Deone and Hugh Evans.

ACKNOWLEDGMENTS

A book like this is never an individual achievement.
Several people, in particular, provided me with
invaluable assistance and I would like to thank them.

John Chambers
Fire and Aviation Management
United States Department of Agriculture
Forest Service

Mariane Davis
Public Information
Park Headquarters
National Park Service
Yellowstone National Park

Mark Mosley
United States Department of Agriculture
Soil Conservation Service

*In the summer of 1988, walls of flames
roared through Yellowstone National Park.*

PROLOGUE:
A VISIT TO YELLOWSTONE

A "moonscape" is how reporters often described the burned land surface of Yellowstone National Park following the great fires of the summer of 1988. It is an odd expression, considering the moon is an airless world of lifeless gray and black soil and rock. Even a square inch of burned-over Yellowstone soil contains more life signs than are known to exist on all the moon. Yet, pictures of the burned areas of Yellowstone gave all who saw them an odd sense of otherworldliness.

Through the summer of 1988, evening news telecasts carried stories about the fires in Yellowstone National Park. Roaring walls of flames 200 feet (60 meters) high, billowing clouds of acrid black smoke, ominous orange-glowing skies, and exhausted and discouraged soot-covered fire fighters filled television screens. Newspaper and magazine headlines shouted "Legacy in Ashes," "Yellowstone Up in Smoke," "Incineration of Yellowstone," and "We Could Have Stopped This." The barrage of fire running across mile upon mile of forest and meadow was matched only by the barrage of sensational news reports. Certainly, the park was lost.

With the fires of 1988 came controversy. Townspeople in the nearby communities soundly denounced park officials for not doing their jobs and stopping the fires when they were small and could be put out easily. Local chambers of commerce bemoaned the loss of millions in tourist dollars. Sports organizations feared for the loss of wildlife habitat and hunting ranges. Park officials countered by saying that all that could be done to suppress the fires was being done. They reported they were managing the largest forest fire-fighting operation in history. Expert fire fighters from the fire lines claimed the Yellowstone fires were unlike anything they had ever fought before, and that it might not be possible to put them out until the exceptionally dry and windy weather changed. Naturalists pronounced fire to be essential to the survival of places like Yellowstone, and that preventing fire would do more harm to the park than good. Fires would create more wildlife habitat than they would destroy and would rejuvenate aging forests of lodgepole pines. Local and national politicians and government officials made fact-finding visits and promised investigations. Against claims and counterclaims, charges and countercharges, was the constant backdrop—walls of fire raging through the woods and over the meadows and dry marshes of Yellowstone.

Television images of wildfire consuming everything in its path filled my mind and I wondered what I would see when my car carried me and my daughter Allison through the east gate and over the 8,500-foot-high (2,584 meters) Sylvan Pass road into the United States' most beloved and revered national park. It was late May 1989, about seven months after the last fires in the Yellowstone National Park were quenched by September rains and the early snows of winter. Would I be stunned and heartbroken to see mile after mile of desolate blackened land with only charred tree skeletons to indicate the past presence of forests? Would I see any of the park's famed wildlife? Would I be angered, as many politicians and local business owners were, by a controversial national park policy that actually let natural fires burn until they extinguished themselves or threatened buildings? Could the fires have been stopped? News accounts of the 1988 fires stated that more than one-half of the 2.2 million acres of trees, meadows, and

*After the fires were out, charred tree
skeletons and controversy remained.*

marshes that comprise this huge park, an area larger than the states of Delaware and Rhode Island combined, had burned. I couldn't imagine how much land that would be. Would Yellowstone look like a giant battle zone where a terrible war was waged?

Battle zone was an apt term. A great battle was fought. At its peak, 9,500 fire fighters, working with hand tools, bulldozers, airplane tankers, helicopters, fire trucks, and high-tech electronics were pitted against a truly awesome force of nature—wildfire.

YELLOWSTONE ON FIRE

Yellowstone National Park, in the northwest corner of Wyoming, encompassing smaller pieces of Montana to the north and Idaho to the southwest, became the first of the U.S. national parks. On March 1, 1872, President Ulysses S. Grant signed the Yellowstone Park Act, creating a "public park and pleasuring-ground." The act prevented homesteaders from moving into the area and dedicated its geyser and hot spring basins, scenic rivers and waterfalls, mountains, huge lakes, vigorous forests, and abundant wildlife "for the benefit and enjoyment of the people."[1] Though many wonderful national parks have since been established across the nation, Yellowstone is a magical name for most people and just about everyone thinks of it as *the* national park. But it is much more than a national park. Yellowstone is an entire region of rivers, forests, and mountain ranges woven together in a mass of interrelationships. Except for the park entry gates and perimeter marker posts, there are no fences or white lines to mark its boundaries and tell you that you have entered the park. The region, called the Greater Yellowstone Area, includes parts of six national forests and two national parks and encompasses several small towns and villages. Grand Teton National Park is located to the south of Yellowstone National Park. All totaled, the Greater Yellowstone Area comprises 11.7 million acres of land—nearly 18,300 square miles (29,409 square km).

The Greater Yellowstone Area is a vast ecosystem of land, water, sky, and living things. Much of the region

13

Beautiful Yellowstone before the raging fires of 1988

lies at an altitude of above 7,000 feet (2,128 meters). Snow piles deep in winter, contributing much moisture to the region, but midsummer brings dryer weather. Yellowstone is famous for its wildlife, including bears, moose, elk, and bison. But even more famous are its geological features—jetting geysers, boiling hot springs, cloud-scraping mountains, deep canyons, and thunderous waterfalls. Not as famous but just as much a part of the ecosystem of the region is wildfire.

Fire is a natural part of the Greater Yellowstone Area. In the latter part of the nineteenth century, a few years before the park was created, fire was commonplace and early visitors to Yellowstone complained of persistent, widespread smoke from fires. The forests were less extensive than they are today. Wildfires kept wide meadows open from the encroachment of trees and shrubs. Much less sagebrush grew across the region. Tree stands ranged widely in maturity, from very young stands to mature ones over two hundred years old.

Yellowstone's natural appearance began to change when the park was created and the land came under human management. In 1886, the U.S. Army was given the job of patrolling its confines and protecting its resources from exploitation. The Army was sent because poachers had been raiding wildlife herds and vandals had seriously damaged its hot-spring formations and other thermal features. In addition to patrols, the Army quickly engaged in the business of forest fire-fighting. A major blaze had begun near the East Fork of the Gardiner River. The fire had raged over a tract of land ten or twelve miles (16 or 19 kilometers) long by three to five miles (5 to 8 kilometers) in width. Inexperienced troops were dispatched to put out the blaze. Their efforts had little effect on the fire and it eventually stopped on its own. The fire was notable only because the Army's suppression efforts were the first attempt by the U.S. government at forest-fire fighting.

By 1916, the Army's role of national park protector came to an end when the National Park Service was created. The new service was instructed to not only "conserve the scenery and the natural and historic objects and the wildlife therein" but also to "provide for the enjoyment of the same in such a manner and by such means as will leave them unimpaired for the enjoyment of future generations."[2] In other words, the National Park Service had two main goals—to provide for preservation of the parks and for their public use. This meant development of policies and programs to protect wildlife, landscape, and forests while creating access roads and park facilities to permit the public the opportunity to see park features. Fire management became one of the Park Service's concerns. However, fire management was often very difficult in Yellowstone National Park because of the rugged nature of the land and the inaccessibility of many of its domains. Except for successful fire suppression efforts in the relatively easily accessible sagebrush and grasslands of the northern domain of the park, fire-suppression activities were not effective until the advent of the airplane as a firefighting tool in the late 1930s and 1940s.

FIRE SEASON

Each summer brings a fire season to Yellowstone. The 1988 fire season began like any other in the park with a lightning strike. On May 24, lightning shattered a cottonwood tree in Lamar Valley, on the eastern side of the park. The tree burned for several hours and then rain came and quenched the flames and glowing embers. The fire was over as simply as that.

Lightning is one of the two major causes of forest fires at Yellowstone as well as anywhere else. In one major study of forest-fire ignitions, it was determined

16

An early fire patrol, in 1923

that lightning started more than 79,000 fires between 1940 and 1975 in the Rocky Mountains alone. In Yellowstone National Park, between 1972 and 1987, lightning strikes ignited at least 269 fires. Most of these fires fizzled out on their own and burned less than an acre. Only a few of the fires ranged over a few hundred or a few thousand acres. The largest natural fire in the historical records for Yellowstone National Park was a fire at Heart Lake in 1931 that eventually burned about 18,000 acres before it was contained by fire fighters.

The other major cause of forest fires is the careless use of fire by human beings. Thoughtless use of smoking materials, campfires not completely put out, sparks from motor vehicles including locomotives, and deliberate burning by arsonists have been responsible for many devastating fires. The largest fire in Yellowstone National Park in 1988 was a human-caused fire.

"LET BURN" POLICY

In 1972, the National Park Service enacted what is sometimes popularly referred to as a "let-burn" policy—or, more accurately, a "natural-burn" policy that permits natural fires falling within the confines of certain conditions to burn naturally as a "prescription." At the urging of ecologists and forest management experts, the Park Service recognized that fires, though infrequent, were just as much a part of normal forest development as rain or snow. Furthermore, in Yellowstone, recent history indicated that most natural fires were relatively small and could be permitted to burn without suppression efforts. When fires are prevented, many forests actually lose their natural character and change. Land protected from fire begins to support non-native species of trees, shrubs, and wildlife that frequent small fires normally keep out. The land is still beautiful but it is different. Furthermore, when large fires come, they can be much larger than they would have been if the small fires had been controlled in the first place. A similar plan was enacted by the Forest Service for some of the wilderness lands under its care.

In the late 1960s and early 1970s, the National Park Service fire management policy allowed the administrators of each national park to develop a fire management plan specific to their own unique conditions. In 1972, Yellowstone National Park administrators formulated a four-part plan. First, the plan permits, as often as possible, lightning-caused fires to burn naturally. Second, the plan calls for fire suppression (fire fighting) if a wildfire threatens people, historic and cultural sites or special natural features; menaces threatened or endangered wildlife; or moves to burn outside park boundaries. Third, the plan calls for full fire suppression on all human-caused fires. When a fire is fought, it is to be done in a manner that is safe for the fire fighters and safe for the park environment. Finally, the plan permits "prescribed" burning in areas where there is excessive buildup of fuels, such as dead and fallen trees. In other words, the decision may be made to deliberately start a fire to use up dangerous fuels so that wildfires cannot later sweep through the area and grow into major conflagrations.

The four-part plan included a major shift for Yellowstone National Park. As fire-fighting techniques and technology had developed, the success rate of fire suppression had climbed. By the early 1970s, many areas of the park had not been touched by fire in more than a hundred years. Downed branches, needles, leaves, and logs—the normal forest debris—were building to a huge accumulation of flammable fuels. Tree stands were reaching maturity and young trees were having difficulty becoming established. Instead of protecting Yel-

Under natural burn policy, fires are allowed to burn.

lowstone and preserving its natural state, fire-suppression efforts were encouraging the buildup of fuels. Fire was needed for a more natural state. Thus, the 1972 "let-burn" policy was established.

From 1972, when the policy was enacted, through 1987, tens of thousands of lightning strikes touched off small fires that quickly withered and died out, usually scorching less than an acre of land. During that time, 235 lightning fires were permitted to burn unchecked, blackening a total of 34,157 acres. The largest natural fire during these sixteen years spread out over 7,400 acres. The policy seemed to be working.

In 1988, the fire season began in the usual way with a lightning strike, but its end would be anything but normal. Fires in the Greater Yellowstone Area that year would grow to historic proportions. The 1988 fire season was unlike anything that had ever been seen there by the seasoned fire fighters brought in from across the country. The wild card that surprised nearly everyone was the weather.

For the six years before 1988, the region had experienced unusually wet summers but winters that were much drier than usual, leading to a general drying of the soils. July rainfall during those years was two to three times greater than normal but was not enough to make up for the winter dryness. The fall of 1987 was also unusually dry for the park region, but caused no real alarm due to the recent trend of higher-than-normal spring and summer rains. Nevertheless, cautious park officials embarked on a daily monitoring program in early April 1988. A number of sites were chosen as representative samples of the entire park. Several measures were taken at each site including determining the moisture content in potential fuels such as trees, pine needles, and decaying leaf duff on the forest floor. Also monitored daily were a "spread component" predicting the ability of a potential fire to move across the landscape, and an "energy release component" estimating how hot a fire would become if ignited. The risk that lightning strikes could start fires and several other fire-related factors were also considered.

By July 1, daily fire-risk monitoring had been extended to twenty-six sites around the park. The data was analyzed by park staff and forest-fire behavior specialists. The fire risk seemed to be within acceptable levels based on the past fire history of the park and expectations of summer rain. As long as fires remained within the conditions outlined in the 1972 park fire management plan, they would be permitted to burn.

In April and May, the weather seemed to be cooperating. April rainfall was 151 percent above normal and May rainfall was 181 percent above normal. However, in June, July, and August a severe drought set in and practically no rain fell during any of those months. It was a summer of drought all across the West. River barges in the Mississippi River were running aground because of a lack of water. In the 112-year recorded history of the park, no summer had ever been this dry. With a fuel moisture content of 8 to 12 percent, lightning easily starts fires. That summer the moisture content of small branches and grasses dropped to as low as 2 to 3 percent. Creeks in the park began to dry up and the Yellowstone River dropped so that the water became scummy and very shallow in places. Even with the low moisture content, the situation was not critical until the winds came.

THE BIG FIRES

The 1988 drought and high winds, sometimes reaching hurricane velocity, nearly doubled the usual number of forest fires in the Greater Yellowstone Area. A total of

249 fires was recorded. Eighty-one percent of those fires were contained at less than 10 acres. The rest accounted for the really massive fires. More than 1.5 million acres, almost 2,500 square miles (4,110 square km), of land in the Greater Yellowstone Area fell within "fire perimeters." But because of the spotty nature of the fires, not all of the land within the perimeters was actually burned. The high winds drove the fire in huge leaps, skipping whole tracts of land to ignite patches of forests acres apart. About 12 percent of the land within the perimeters totally escaped fire. Large areas received only light surface burns. Within the park itself, just less than 1 million acres of land, not quite half the park's total acreage, was burned during the summer.

The 1988 fires of unprecedented scale within the Greater Yellowstone Area were met with the largest fire-suppression efforts in history. More than 25,000 fire fighters fought fires there during the season. Fire fighters operated 100 fire engines and used 117 aircraft to transport fire crews and supplies and to apply thousands of dumps of water and chemical fire retardants to attempt to quench flames. Helicopters dropped 11.4 million gallons of fire retardants and water. By the fire season's end, the total cost came to approximately $120 million. In spite of the effort, many residents of the area were angered by the fire-suppression's "ineffectiveness." Don Edgarton, manager of the photo shop at the Old Faithful tourist complex, said: "They're [fire crews] going around the campgrounds saving restrooms and old cabins. We've got 10 million trees that are gone. They ain't saving none of them. . . . We're sick about what's happened to the forest because we don't believe its going to come back in three, four or five years."[3] Fire Incident Commander of the North Fork Fire denied that his crews just let the trees burn. "We have fought this fire aggressively from day one. . . .

*As fires approached Old Faithful,
the U.S. Army was called in to
help clear fuel from a fire line.*

Only a mile-wide fire line could have stopped the fire storm from spotting at Old Faithful and burning the ridgeline beyond the observation point."[4]

When fire lines are constructed to stop the advance of fire by removing burnable fuels, the land is scraped clean of all vegetation down to bare mineral soil. A fire line one mile wide would have been even more destructive than a fire. In fact, it is not clear that a one-mile-wide fire line would have stopped the fire storm. High winds driving fires all through the park routinely spotted new fires up to one and a half miles ahead of their fronts by lofting glowing embers and even burning branches. Traditional barriers to forest fires such as roads and rivers were of little effect on some of the Yellowstone fire fronts. Fires were even able to jump major topographic features such as the Grand Canyon of Yellowstone to spot new fires on the opposite rim!

From the above figures, and public anger surrounding the episode, it would be easy to conclude that the 1988 fire season destroyed nearly half of Yellowstone National Park. But figures and angry feelings, especially in regard to forest fires, can be misleading. What actually happened to the park is much more complicated. In fact, many "destroyed" areas were not destroyed at all!

---

1. Utley, R. M. (1982), "National Parks," *American History Illustrated,* v. 17, n. 1, p. 17.
2. Ibid., p. 18.
3. Simpson, R. W. (1988), "The Fires of '88, Yellowstone Park & Montana in Flames," *American Geographic Publishing Montana Magazine,* p. 11.
4. Ibid.

GRANDFATHER FIRE

[Forests] only await a spark of fire to give rise to one of the wildest scenes of destruction of which the world is capable. When the fire has once started, the pitchy trees burn rapidly; the flames rush through their tops and high above them with a roaring noise. Should the atmosphere be calm, the ascending heat soon causes the air to flow in, and after a time the wind acquires great velocity. An irresistible front of flame is soon developed, and it sweeps forward, devouring the forest before it like the dry grass in a running prairie fire, which this resembles, but on a gigantic scale. The irregular line of fire has a height of a hundred feet or more above the trees, or two hundred from the ground. Great sheets of flame appear to disconnect themselves from the fiery torrent and leap upward and explode, or dart forward, bridging over open spaces such as lakes and rivers, and starting the fire afresh in advance of the main column, as if impatient of the slower progress which it is making. These immense shooting flames are probably due to the large quantities of inflammable gas evolved from the heated tree tops just in advance of actual combustion, and they help to account for the almost incredible speed of some of the larger forest fires, one of which was known to run about 130 miles in twelve hours, or upwards of ten miles per hour.

Robert Bell
*Assistant Director of the Canadian
Geological Survey* 1889[1]

Fire, as a force in nature, has immense importance for humans. Though frequently regarded negatively, as in the burning of a building or in a forest fire, fire is often very beneficial to humans. We use it for many forms of transportation, heating, cooking, electric power generation, manufacturing, and agriculture. The control of fire is one of the major factors in the emergence of modern humanity from its cave-dwelling ancestry.

Fire is a force that inspires fear and respect. Native Americans of many Indian nations referred to fire as "Grandfather Fire" to show their great reverence. They used fire for more than just heating their dwellings and cooking their food. When hunting, Indians would sometimes ignite grasslands and shrubby areas to drive out rabbits so they could be caught more easily. Forest lands were torched to open clearings. In a year or two, those clearings were filled with excellent browse that attracted deer and other big game. So common was the practice of clearing woods by fire that the Europeans who came to the New World often settled there. Plains Indians set fire to grasslands so that succulent new spring growth would attract bison. Some Indians protected their prairie villages from wildfire by burning off the grass covering of large areas of land and then settling in the middle of the scorched area. Indians also used fire in warfare. Osbourn Russell, a nineteenth-century fur trapper of the Yellowstone region, was once attacked by a war party of Blackfeet Indians. He wrote in his journal that Indians set fire to nearby vegetation to drive him and his companions out of hiding.

WHAT IS FIRE?

Forest fires are complex heat engines. Their magnitude is determined by a number of factors that make it very difficult to predict what they will do and to control them. The extent of wildfires is determined by the nature of the fuel they burn through, the arrangement of the fuel and its moisture content, climatic and micro-climatic conditions, topography, and air humidity. Successful wildfire suppression is much more than just backbreaking work. It is a science that depends upon a detailed understanding of just what fire is and how it works.

Fire is a rapid chemical reaction that takes place in the presence of heat and in which oxygen combines with elements such as carbon. Fire is actually a decomposition process because, through it, complex chemical compounds are recombined into simpler compounds such as carbon monoxide and carbon dioxide. Forest fuels, including wood, pine needles, and leaf litter, contain a variety of hydrocarbon (hydrogen and carbon) compounds. Some of these compounds, like cellulose and lignin, provide structure and stiffness for wood. Also found in wood, leaves, and needles are varying quantities of other materials like terpenes—that give piney woods their characteristic smell on warm days—and waxes, oils, resins, and water. During fire, water is driven off and hydrocarbon compounds break down and combine with free oxygen to form simpler carbon compounds. The process releases great quantities of heat that carry the fire reaction to new, unburned fuels.

FIRE TRIANGLE

Fire requires three components—fuel, oxygen, and heat. In forests the fuel is a carbon compound like wood, pine needles, or leaves. Oxygen is supplied by the atmosphere. The air we breathe is composed of 78 percent nitrogen and approximately 21 percent oxygen. The remaining 1 percent includes a variety of gases such as carbon dioxide and water vapor. In certain kinds of fires, oxygen is not supplied by the atmosphere; it is supplied by the chemicals reacting together during burning. Gunpowder is a good example.

The third component of fire is heat. In order to begin, the chemical reaction that is fire usually requires a large heat input many times greater than normal surface temperatures on earth. This is fortunate, for otherwise fires would ignite in suitable fuels constantly. During burning, additional heat is released by the chemical reaction and this provides the heat necessary for other fuels to burn.

Fire-fighter manuals often describe fuel, oxygen, and heat as the three corners of a *fire triangle*. All three are required for a fire to burn. If any one of the three corners of the triangle is removed, the fire will go out. All fire fighting is based on this idea. Forest fire fighters spend much of their time on the fire line trying to remove fuel in front of a fire. They create fire lines by scraping and cutting away with hand tools or bulldozers all living or dead vegetation down to the mineral soil. When the fire front arrives at the fire line, it simply runs out of fuel to burn and goes out. Fire fighters also spray water on burning materials or shovel dirt on them to smother the fire and cut off its oxygen supply, and to cool down the burning materials below the temperature necessary to sustain the fire.

FIRE BEHAVIOR

Of great concern to fire scientists who study the nature of fire and to fire fighters who must put out fires is *fire behavior*. This refers to the manner in which a wildfire develops. Two factors control this development. The first is *ignition*, which is the heating of a material until the chemical process of fire begins. Another factor is *fire spread*, or the way the fire moves through various

29

fuels. Each factor is affected, in turn, by numerous variables.

Ignition

In forest fires, the fire process can be thought of as the thermal degradation of wood, leaves, needles, and various grasses that may be present. Wood, for example, begins to change markedly when its temperature approaches 212 degrees Fahrenheit (100 degrees Celsius), the boiling point of water. Free moisture within the wood begins to boil away at the surface, while moisture beneath the surface is driven inward toward the center of the wood. Between about 260 degrees and 370 degrees Fahrenheit (127 to 188 degrees Celsius), lignins begin to degrade depending upon how much moisture is still present in the wood. Above 400 degrees Fahrenheit (204 degrees Celsius), the degradation of lignin becomes rapid. As the temperature of the wood rises still higher to about 530 degrees Fahrenheit (277 degrees Celsius), wood loses about 35 percent of its weight. Cellulose fibers begin to break down. Complex chemicals in the wood start releasing flammable gas. Beyond this temperature, the ignition or flaming point of the released gases is reached and flames are produced. Still higher, at temperatures between about 930 and 1,100 degrees Fahrenheit (499 to 593 degrees Celsius), the wood surface itself begins to glow.

By the time all the wood is used up by fire reaction, all that is left is a powdery mineral-rich ash. It is tempting to conclude that the fire has consumed the wood. This is not so. The fire has instead changed the wood into different forms. Much of the wood has been changed into water vapor, gases, tar, and soot that have risen into the atmosphere. The total quantity of matter in the wood has remained the same, but much of it has now spread out into the atmosphere.

Fire Spread

Fire spread is the way fire develops and moves through various fuels. It is influenced by the amount of fuel available for burning, the weather—particularly the wind—and the shape of the land. (Much more will be said about this later.) How a fire spreads is of great concern to fire fighters who are charged with protecting property and life. If a fire has to be fought, attack lines have to be established in the direction it will move. If a fire line is set up in the wrong place and the fire moves off in a new direction, all efforts will have been wasted and the fire may become a major conflagration.

Heat Transfer

In order for fire to spread, heat must be transferred from burning material to nonburning material. Heat transfer takes place in three ways: *conduction, convection,* and *radiation*. If you have ever picked up a hot iron skillet from a stove, you know about conduction, which is a direct passage of heat through the material being heated. The molecules of the material being heated increase their movement or vibrations at the point where the heat is applied. These movements are then transferred by bumping or colliding with the molecules next to them. These molecules, in turn, cause molecules next to them to increase their vibrations, and so on. Heat is thereby conducted or moved through the material being heated. This is why the handle of an iron skillet can get very hot even though it is not directly in a flame.

Conduction is not a very efficient heat-transfer process in wood. The unburned end of a log in a campfire can be picked up safely without burning your hand even though the other end has been on fire for an hour. Nevertheless, conduction is important in fire because it moves heat from the outside to the inside of logs and branches to preheat them as the outside burns. Preheating of log and branch interiors drives off moisture and begins the degradation process that the flames will eventually finish. However, the outside has to burn for quite some time before the inside is burned as well. In many forest fires, the fire moves so quickly through tree stands that only the outside layers of the trees are charred. If the fire has killed the trees, but not destroyed the wood, logging companies may be permitted to remove the dead but still usable timber.

Convection is another powerful heat transfer force during forest fires. It is a process that occurs in liquids and gases in which they physically carry the heat away from the heat source. Although convection in liquid does not play a significant part in heat transfer in forest fires, it is the kind of convection we are most familiar with. The soup in a pot on a hot stove develops convection currents. The heated soup at the bottom expands slightly and becomes less dense than the cooler soup at the top. The hot soup is buoyant and it rises or is convected to the top. The cooler soup falls to the pot bottom, becomes heated, and it too begins to rise in a circular current. Convection in gas works the same way.

The heat released by a wildfire helps to sustain burning by causing the released gas to expand in volume. Some of these gases are flammable and ignite in flames to expand even more. Like the heated soup, the heated gases within the flaming area become buoyant in the surrounding cooler air in the nonflaming areas and they rise or float upward. This upward convection current carries the combustion-product gases away. By removing so much gas, the convection current produces a low-pressure zone within the flaming area. Outside air immediately floods in and provides a fresh supply of oxygen to sustain combustion as well as to fan the fire and to continue to drive off waste gases.

Convection currents from a forest fire can produce huge, billowing clouds of black smoke that may rise thousands of feet in the air to blot out the sun and create twilight or nightlike conditions on the ground in the middle of the day. Very strong ground winds will rush into the fire, be heated, and continue the upward convection current. In hilly or mountainous areas, convection will carry heated gases upslope to trees that haven't caught fire yet. The gases will preheat the unburned trees almost to their ignition temperature. When the flames reach the preheated trees, they immediately ignite. In extreme conditions, the trees may even burst into flames on their own before flames from other trees reach them. Under these circumstances, wildfires can race upslope and engulf several miles of forest an hour.

Radiation is the third heat transfer process. It is the process by which your hands get warmed when you hold them in front of a crackling fire on a cold day. Radiation can carry heat in any direction through the air or even through outer space. Radiation is the manner in which the sun's energy reaches Earth. The heat radiated around a wildfire is tremendous and can encourage the spread of the fire by preheating nearby unburned fuels. However, most radiant heat from a forest fire is simply lost directly to outer space.

Fuels

Perhaps more than any other factor determining the extent of a wildfire is the nature of the materials fire is burning through. Not all fuels are alike. Their variations in composition, size, and moisture content greatly affect their burning. How much fuel is actually present is another major concern. Grass, for example, normally produces about ¼ to 1 ton of fuel per acre of land. If the land is covered with sagebrush, the amount of fuel present can range from 2 to 5 tons per acre. Second-growth timber—trees that have replaced old-growth timber following logging operations—totals somewhere between 100 and 600 tons per acre. Finally, mature timber—trees that have been left untouched for a very

*A fire fighter uses a chain saw to clear
possible fuel from a fire line.*

long time—weigh in at between 200 and 600 tons per acre.[2] When a tract of land is sparsely covered with fuel, the fire has little potential for spreading, regardless of the kind of fuel present. On the other hand, the more fuel available to burn, the greater the fire can become. Furthermore, land with heavy fuel loads can be subject to more than one episode of fire during an incident. A fire may sweep through a wooded tract and burn off the ground cover of grass, small shrubs, and dead branches and scorch tree trunks. Later, the fire may reach an area where dead branches are still attached to trees or smaller trees are growing next to taller ones. The dead branches or small trees can carry the fire up to the crown of the trees. A *crown fire* may result in which the tops of trees burn and the fire may then sweep back, if winds help, through the areas previously burned on the ground to finish the job.

Fuel size and compactness are important to the spread of a fire. If you have ever made a campfire during an outing or built a fire in a fireplace, you will know why these two factors are important. Unless they are very dry, heavy logs are difficult to start burning. They contain a lot of moisture that has to be driven away by heat before ignition can take place. Small-diameter fuels contain much less moisture, so it is easier to elevate their temperatures to the ignition point. Moisture in fuels increases the amount of heating necessary before ignition can take place. This effect can be demonstrated by placing a small amount of water in the bottom of a paper cup and holding the cup over a candle flame. The water absorbs the heat applied to the cup and carries it off through increased evaporation. The paper-cup bottom will not become hot enough to ignite until the water is gone. Moisture in logs performs the same function. The surface of the wood must be heated to drive away the moisture before ignition temperature can be reached.

A good fire builder starts with small-diameter fuels at the bottom and places larger-diameter fuels at the top. The small fuels start readily and the heat they produce rises by convection to preheat the larger-diameter fuels on top. Eventually, moisture in the larger fuels will be driven away, chemicals and fibers in the wood will begin breaking down, and their surface temperatures will rise to the ignition point. Wildfires normally start in small fuels and spread to larger fuels if sufficient heat is present.

Fuel compactness also affects campfires and wildfires. If you try to build a fire by laying logs tightly together, the air gaps between the logs will be very small. Fire gases, fresh oxygen, and even heat simply cannot circulate freely around the logs. The fire will burn slowly, if at all. In a successful campfire, the wood is placed in a crisscross or tepee fashion rather than being stacked tightly. This arrangement permits oxygen to reach and sustain many burning surfaces at a time, yielding a very hot fire. In a forest fire, loosely stacked accumulations of branches on the forest floor will burn very rapidly. Tightly packed needles and leaves burn slowly. A lighted cigarette butt carelessly tossed into forest floor duff may ignite the tightly packed duff and, if wind conditions are low, the fire can smolder and snake through the duff for hours before finally going out. Only if the fire reaches a better fuel, like a pile of branches, or if the wind conditions pick up, will the fire take off.

Fuel chemistry is another significant factor in how fuel burns. Each kind of fuel has a unique chemistry. Fuels like wood are composed of varying amounts of cellulose (mostly water and glucose), lignin, oils, waxes, resins, turpines, and minerals. Cellulose fiber makes up about 75 percent of wood. Lignin comprises 15 percent, and the remaining constituents make up about 10 percent. Grasses are predominantly cellulose fiber and when dry are light in mass and burn quickly. Trees and shrubs like eucalyptus and chamise have high concentrations of flammable resins that, if dry, nearly explode when they come in contact with fire.

Still another fuel factor in the spread of fire is the age and health of trees and other vegetation. Trees, in particular, are very susceptible to fire when, for their species, they are old. Old trees have many dead branches, either still attached or accumulated on the ground, that can sustain a fire. Insect infestations and diseases will have damaged protective bark and weakened trunks and branches. Wind storms and winter ice storms add to the damage. During dry conditions, wildfires have a fairly easy time moving through stands of old trees.

Young trees, although retaining higher amounts of moisture than older trees, can be susceptible to fire during a dry season. When young, their canopies of branches are still close to the ground; grass fires racing through stands of young trees can wipe them out quickly. Mature trees offer the greatest resistance to fire. Unless the flames can climb up to the canopy of branches to begin a crown fire, forest fires usually do little damage to stands of mature trees. The protective bark covering may be scorched but the growing wood inside is undamaged. Needles and leaves will brown out from the heat carried up to them by convection currents but future growth will replace them. Naturalists actually believe that a ground fire can be beneficial to mature trees because it clears accumulated debris at their bases and can fireproof the stand (make it less susceptible to fire) for a long time. Because the fire increases decomposition of forest-floor debris, nutrients are released that are used by the mature trees for continued growth.

Heat Value

During combustion, the amount of heat released is determined by the nature of the materials being burned.

Each kind of fuel has its own *heat value,* which is the ability of that fuel to give off heat during complete combustion. The heat is measured in BTUs, or British thermal units, which is defined as the amount of heat necessary to raise the temperature of 1 pound of water 1 degree Fahrenheit. That is about the amount of heat you would get if you burned a 1-square-inch piece of newspaper. Gasoline and fuel oil have heat values in the range of 24,500 BTUs per pound. Forest fuels like wood are estimated to have heat values of between 6,300 and 8,000 BTUs. In a really big forest fire, like the 1988 fires at Yellowstone National Park, during the times of maximum intensity heat was released at about 3 trillion BTUs per square mile of burning timber. This amount of energy release is enough to heat 4,300 homes for a full year. In really hot fires, like the 1967 Sundance Fire in the panhandle of Idaho, the energy released every two minutes equaled that of the atom bomb dropped on Hiroshima in World War II.[3]

Weather

As seen from the earlier discussion, the nature of fuel the fire is burning through is very important to the fire spreading. Different fuels burn at different rates and intensities. When the fuel is just right, fire will race through it and spread over large areas. Many other factors may influence flame development. One of the most important is weather.

Fires spread most efficiently in dry weather. Rain and snow can cool burning fuels to below the ignition temperature and smother them so that oxygen has a difficult time reaching the burning surface. To be effective, however, rain or snow has to fall in sufficient quantities and must last for several hours or days. Because of hot, upward convection currents, light rain or snow may never reach the ground. During big fires, rising heat simply evaporates the rain or snow before it reaches the flames. If you have poured water on a campfire that has burned for several hours, you might have been surprised at the amount of water needed to put it completely out. Until the charred logs cool, much of the water flashes into steam. Hot spots that the water did not reach may remain, and stirring and turning over the logs will be necessary to extinguish all the glowing embers. Likewise, an intense but short cloudburst will cool a big fire down, but it won't necessarily put it out. Hot spots are likely to flare up and continue the fire.

Temperature is a powerful determinant of fire spread. Wildfires rarely start or achieve any significance in the northern regions during winter. If fuels are chilled down to below the freezing point of water, it is hard for a spark to raise the temperature of the fuel to the ignition point. Assuming a wintry day of 0 degrees Fahrenheit (-18 degrees Celsius), the fuel's temperature will have to be raised to approximately 600 degrees Fahrenheit (316 degrees Celsius) to achieve ignition. However, the fuel's temperature will have to be raised only to about 450 degrees Fahrenheit (232 degrees Celsius) on a hot summer day when the air temperature is 100 degrees Fahrenheit (38 degrees Celsius). On such days, the temperature of surface material can climb to about 150 degrees Fahrenheit (66 degrees Celsius). Remember walking barefoot across an asphalt street or playground on a hot summer day?

Humidity in the air also exerts a strong influence on flame development. Air moisture and moisture in wood and other fuels are related. Fuels dry out when exposed to dry air for an appreciable time. Fuel moisture simply evaporates. If humidity remained low for several months, even thick logs might dry out and the moisture in the air and in the logs would equalize. This doesn't often happen because air moisture changes constantly during the day and over weeks. Light fuels like grass do respond very quickly to changes in humidity. Grass fires in desert regions of Arizona will go out by themselves if the humidity in the air rises to 20 percent.[4]

There is a time lag between changes in air humidity and changes in the moisture content of wood. The lag is the amount of time it takes moisture to enter or leave the fuel. Fuel with a diameter of less than ¼ inch has a 1-hour lag. Fuel ranging from ¼ inch to 1 inch in diameter lags about 10 hours behind air humidity changes. The time lag for fuel from 1 to 3 inches is about 100 hours, and fuel 3 to 8 inches or more lags about 1,000 hours behind air humidity.[5] When air humidity drops very low, small-diameter fuels are ready to burn about an hour later. Large-diameter fuels (3 to 8 inches) require a consistent low-humidity pattern over weeks or months to become dangerously ready for ignition. Moisture content in these large-diameter fuels is labeled "1,000-hour fuel moisture." When very low, it is a strong indicator of drought conditions. In the Greater Yellowstone Area, the 1988 long-term drought ultimately reduced the 1,000-hour fuel moisture from the normal 16 to 20 percent to 2 to 3 percent.

Humidity will drop during the heat of the day and climb during the cool of the night, but not always. In the long run, humidity follows trends based on seasonal air temperature, the amount of rainfall that has fallen, and winds. Usually when a dry season sets in, air temperature climbs and fuel begins to dry out. The fire danger is great. During a wet season, fire danger drops dramatically. If a wildfire does start, it tends to grow and spread and become very intense between 10 A.M. and 6 P.M. This is when the air temperature is highest—encouraging preheating of fuels—and when humidity is generally lowest. In the evening, night, and early-morning hours, fires tend to "lie down," or burn with less intensity because of lower air temperatures and higher humidity. This is when fire fighters find suppression efforts are most effective. In the unusual Yellowstone weather conditions of 1988, humidity remained low even at night.

Wind is another meteorological factor in flame development. On calm days, flames simply rise upward and the fire front expands very slowly in all directions. The fire spreads mainly because of preheating caused by radiant heat transfer. This kind of fire is relatively easy to put out, as the fire fighters have time to completely encircle the fire with fire lines. Furthermore, the lack of wind reduces the possibility of the fire spotting, or spreading by starting small new fires from the glowing embers thrown beyond the fire line.

Winds fan fires and cause them to race through fuel. Strong winds can bend flames almost parallel to the ground. The winds help drive convection currents horizontally so that preheating of unburned fuels takes place more rapidly and the flames spread more quickly. Rather than spreading slowly in all directions at once, the flames move in the same direction as the wind.

Fire fighting at Yellowstone in 1988 was plagued by high winds that sometimes reached hurricane force. Frequent wind speeds of 60 mph (97 kph) blew the flames horizontally. The winds were a combination of natural winds passing through the area and winds produced by tremendous convection currents developed by the fires. Extremely hot fires sent heated gases and smoke thousands of feet upward. New oxygen-rich air rushed in from the sides to fill the partial void left by the convection currents. The flames grew hotter and increased the convection currents, which increased the wind flow, and so on. Terrifying wailing, rumbling firestorms raced through the Yellowstone woods, disintegrating everything flammable in their path. In addition to driving the flames, the wind also cast firebrands miles ahead of the storm. In these conditions, fires can move extremely fast. In 1921, the Matilija Fire in southern California dashed 15 miles (24 kilometers) in just an hour. Wind-driven fire advances of 5 to 10 miles (8 to 16 kilometers) per hour are not uncommon, and firebrands have been known to have been blown more than 10 miles (16 kilometers) to spot other fires.

Topography

Topography, or the shape of the land, also has a strong influence on flame development. Flatland fires either spread out evenly in all directions or are blown by the wind in a particular direction. Fires on sloped land nearly always travel upslope. The reason for this is twofold and fairly simple. Hold a lighted wooden match horizontally and watch the fire move slowly along the wood toward your fingers. Hold the match so that the lighted end is downward, and your fingers immediately feel the heat as the fire quickly spreads toward the unburned wood. Sloped land, especially steeply sloped land, promotes upslope development of the flaming fire front. Fuels preheat more rapidly on sloped land than on level ground. Consequently, fires tend to race uphill, especially if wind is blowing in that direction also. Wind frequently blows uphill. Winds along flatlands are directed upward by sloped land. The upward slope acts almost as a chimney, producing a strong updraft that promotes upward fire spread.

Slope of the land is especially critical in flame spread when the slope is part of a steep-walled valley or canyon. Fire approaching the valley or canyon from the lower end can be driven upslope almost explosively. Again, the upward end of a valley or canyon will act as a fireplace chimney does to produce a strong updraft. Fires in such places are dangerous for fire fighters and wildlife because it is easy to become trapped by the flames on the upslope end. At nighttime, however,

The fire front tends to race uphill on sloped land.

these fires have a strong tendency to die down. Valleys and canyons cool off quickly at night and their steep walls tend to accumulate smoke from the fire, keeping out fresh air. It is not until late in the morning, when the sun clears the valley ridges, that the wind can again pick up and flush out the smoky air.

Sometimes, lightning starts fires on mountainous ridges and highlands. There is nowhere for the fire to go but downslope. Development of the flame is similar to the way flames develop when a lighted match is held with the flaming end upward. They burn very slowly down the matchstick. Without strong winds, flames merely creep downslope. On occasion, spotting well down-slope may take place when burning pine cones or other debris roll downhill and start new fires. In that case, the uphill fire continues to work its way down and meets the spot fires working their way up.

Fire Spread

The last important component of fire behavior is fire spread. This is the manner in which fire spreads hori-zontally and vertically. Fire spread depends on the con-tinuity of the fuel bed, fuel loading or how much fuel is available in tons per acre, and the arrangement and size and shape of the fuel.

Continuity of fuel beds is an important factor. A continuous fuel bed, one in which the fuel type and size stays constant, permits the fire to grow to its maximum potential. When fuel changes over distance, the fire may pick up or diminish in pace. For example, a fire burn-ing from brush into a grassy area will at least double its rate of spread across the grass. Grass is a much lighter fuel than brush and therefore it requires less heating to reach the ignition point. So, a relatively slow-moving brush fire will begin to race when it hits grass. Conversely, a grass fire will slow down its rate of spread to one-half if it moves into brush.[6]

The arrangement and the size of the fuel greatly affect the ability of the fire to spread. Fuel packed together tightly will slow combustion because the packing reduces the fuel surface area that can be preheated at one time and impedes the flow of oxygen needed to sustain the combustion process. Fuel size is simply the diameter of the fuel. Thick logs and branches require more preheating before ignition can take place than thin diameter fuels like twigs, needles, and grasses.

Fire fighters are very concerned about potential fire spread. Increased suppression efforts, including air strikes with water from helicopters or bombers, may be called for if it is determined that a fire might accelerate because it is moving into a faster burning fuel.

FIRE TYPES

Not all wildfires are alike. Some fires barely mar the sky with smoke before they fizzle out on their own. Others sweep over the landscape like giant tornadoes of flame, incinerating everything burnable in their path. Still others fall somewhere between these two extremes. In general, there are three patterns of fire; the extent of each is determined by local conditions such as fuel availability and weather.

Ground Fires

Ground fires creep along the ground in compacted fuels like leaf and pine needle duff and peat moss. These fires burn slowly and do not yield much heat. Ground fires can be smoky for their size because of incomplete combustion of fuels. Compared to other fires, ground fires do not exhibit much flaming and, instead, sustain themselves for hours by glowing. This kind of fire looks like a campfire that has burned down so that only hot, glowing coals are left.

Surface Fires

A ground fire can snake in an erratic pattern in all directions through the forest floor duff for hours but— if it reaches an area where there is an accumulation of dry branches or uncompacted leaves and pine needles, or meets low-to-the-ground dry shrubs and dry grass— it can become a surface fire. Because these surface fuels are usually open and not compacted like forest-floor duff, surface fires burn much more quickly and give off much more heat as well. The fire moves through the fuel with a flaming front and, if wind is present, the flames will be fanned and bent toward the ground so that preheating of unburned fuels in the direction the wind is blowing is accelerated. Surface fires do minimal damage to trees. At worst, the bark at the base of trees will be charred and burned through in places where dry branches or fallen tree trunks came to rest next to them. In those instances, the downed fuel, while burning itself, kept the flames at the base of the tree for a long enough time to permit burn-through.

Crown Fire

The worst fire pattern is the crown fire. When they take place they are the most destructive of fires and certainly the most terrifying. If a *fire ladder* is present, flames from a surface fire can climb to the canopies of trees and erupt in violent and often erratic surges. Fire ladders are trees with dead and dry branches still clinging to their trunks, or small trees near the base of taller trees.

Like the continuous rumbling of a heavy freight train,

Flames sweeping up through tree branches create a crown fire.

crown fires roar as they tear and burn their way through forests. Driven by strong winds often of their own creation, flames leap from treetop to treetop at speeds of 10 miles (16 kilometers) or more per hour. Especially violent crown fires are called *fire storms*. Swirling, inward-flowing winds, filling the voids left by powerful upward convection currents, can be so strong that the tops of thick trees will snap off and be sucked into the tornadolike inferno. Firebrands as thick as a person's arm are blown miles ahead of the fire's advance, spotting new fires. Thick, black smoke blots out the sun, turning day into night. Flames race up and down rugged terrain at speeds faster than people can run. Fire storms have been known to kill hundreds of people in just minutes and destroy entire villages as they sweep through. These fires are so hot, little is left behind them. Faint white streaks of powdery ash are all that remain to indicate trees were once present. Forest-fire fighters call fire storms "blowups."

WHO DONE IT?

By and large, human beings are responsible for most fires in the world. Many human-caused fires are deliberate, as in the case of slash-and-burn agriculture. In developing nations of the world, especially in regions like the tropical rain forests of Brazil, exploding populations and the need for economic development are eating away forest lands. Farmers move into tropical forests and cut down hundreds of acres of forests at a time. Timber is heaped on the ground and fire is set to clear the land. The air pollution produced by slash-and-burn techniques is formidable. Space Shuttle astronauts have had difficulty seeing certain South American countries because of the amount of smoke produced by hundreds or thousands of agricultural fires. Unfortunately, the land cleared is often of poor quality and after a few years of crops, it no longer has the nutrients to support agriculture. The farmers move on and repeat the process somewhere else, leaving a broad path of depleted, almost barren soil behind them.

In the United States some ranchers often employ prescribed burning to clear rangeland of unwanted cedar and juniper trees and sagebrush, and to stimulate lush new grass growth in the spring. Prescribed fires are used when the conditions are right to stimulate forest growth and remove unwanted species. California giant sequoias are periodically subjected to fire to burn off Douglas firs that might serve as fire ladders and carry wildfires to the sequoia crowns. Without the Douglas firs, sequoias can survive repeated burnings.

Many human-caused fires are accidental, started by careless use of smoking materials and failure to properly extinguish campfires. Other fires are caused by arsonists who, for various reasons, set incendiary devices to ignite woods and grasslands.

Most wildfires in the United States are caused by lightning strikes. Around the world there are more than 40,000 lightning storms each day. Every second at least 100 lightning bolts strike. That amounts to more than 8.5 million strikes a day.

Lightning strikes are normally of two kinds. "Cold strokes" pack an intense current but have a short duration. Cold strokes tend to explode things. The moisture in a tree hit by a cold stroke will instantly boil and overpressurize the tree's interior, causing it to blast apart in large wooden shards. "Hot strokes" have less current but last longer before dissipating. Hot strokes cause more heating than cold strokes, and are more likely to start fires. In the United States, between 1940 and 1975, lightning strikes have been responsible for nearly 90,000 fires in California and the Pacific Northwest alone.

Lightning, by itself, however, is not enough to start

*Lightning strikes are a frequent
cause of forest fires.*

fires. Most lightning strikes take place in the tropical areas of the world, but few fires there are started by lightning. The climate is simply too moist for lightning to have much effect. As with all other forms of fire ignition, dry conditions and plenty of available fuel are important to fire development.

Though lightning-caused fires are very common in the United States, most lightning fires do not cause much damage. About 80 percent of lightning fires burn no more than 10 acres of land. About 2 to 3 percent of all fires, lightning or human-caused, account for 95 percent of the annual burn area in the United States.

FIRE DANGER RATING

If you have ever traveled through U.S. national forests, most likely you have passed signs that indicated the current danger of fire. These signs are reminders to forest users and tourists to exercise caution when handling fire, especially smoking material. The signs are updated daily for weather and moisture conditions of the forest. Five classes or conditions are recognized for fire danger.[7]

Low danger. Fires do not start readily from most accidental causes, though many lightning fires may start in some areas during low-danger periods. Fires that do start generally spread slowly and show little tendency to spot. They often do not burn clean, but spread in irregular fingers.

Medium Danger. Fires can start from most accidental causes, but the number of starts is generally low. Rate of spread of fires is moderate; heavy concentrations of fuel will burn hot, and there may be some spotting. Control of fires during this period usually presents no special problems.

51

High Danger. Fires will start easily from most causes. They will burn hot, spread rapidly, and spot readily. Control of fires may become difficult, unless they are hit hard and fast while small.

Very High Danger. Fires start easily from most causes. They will develop quickly and can spread at high rates of speed with considerable spotting. Direct attack at the head of a fire is rarely possible after it has been burning a few minutes.

Extreme Danger. Fires start easily from all causes and may be started by unusual or unexpected causes. They burn intensely and spread rapidly. Direct attack is rarely possible except when fires are still small. The running heads of large fires are usually uncontrollable while the extreme danger period lasts and most effective control work must be confined to the flanks of the fires and to well-planned strategy.

It can be seen from these five classes of fire danger that no time is completely safe from wildfire. Caution should always be exercised when handling fire. In February, before the big blowups at Yellowstone, a few back-country skiers in the Gallatin National Forest lit a lunch fire on top of a snowbank. The skiers left the fire burning and in a few hours the snow beneath had melted through. The woods were so dry that the fuels beneath the snow ignited and the ensuing fire charred one-tenth of an acre of trees before going out.

"WEIRD" FIRES [8]

One would think that forest fire fighters had seen everything when a well-meaning backpacker tried to dispose of toilet paper by burning it and inadvertently started one of the Greater Yellowstone Area 1988 fires.

Actually, the toilet paper fire is less strange than many others. Most forest fires are started by lightning, careless use of smoking materials, runaway campfires, or arson, but there are a few really odd ignitions, like the two-acre fire started by a pig on a ranch near Oroville, California. The ranch owner was disposing of trash when the pig ran up and snatched a piece of burning paper and dashed through dry grass with it.

Animals have been blamed for quite a few forest fires. A bear is said to have started a blaze in Mt. Baker National Forest in Washington. The starting point of the blaze was traced back to a fisherman's backpack the bear had stolen. Apparently, while rummaging through the pack for good things to eat, the bear caused some matches to rub together and ignite. Birds have also been blamed for starting fires. Some have been known to pick up unextinguished cigarette butts and carry them off to use as nesting material. Near La Crosse, Wisconsin, on the banks of the Mississippi River, a group of men were trying to contain a bottomland fire. Panicked pheasants took off from the fire zone with their tail feathers on fire. On occasion, the fur of small animals has been ignited by forest fires. Fire fighters working fire lines have seen their control efforts thwarted as the animals ran across the line and inadvertently ignited other woods. Beavers were blamed for a forest fire in the northern Sierra region of California when they felled a tree across a power line. The resulting short circuit showered sparks below, igniting the blaze.

Then, there is a story of a flaming goat. A sheepherder was trying to cure a goat of mange, a skin disease caused by small mites that get into an animal's coat. The animal suffers from itching, sores, and loss of fur. The sheepherder poured kerosene on the goat to kill the mites. The frightened goat ran off, passing by the sheepherder's campfire. The goat's coat ignited and the animal left a trail of fire as it ran through the woods.

Strange human-caused fires are also common. Dur-

53

ing a local election in Arkansas, a politician decided to boost his campaign by destroying a rival's poster tacked to a tree. Instead of simply tearing it down, the politician burned it off and torched the tree as well. In California, a ranchhand started an 80-acre fire after hearing local stories of a gas seep coming up from the ground. He found a hole in the ground with gas seeping up, and tried to get a better look by lighting a match. You can imagine the result.

Two men from New York started a campfire in South Dakota to keep warm. The fire got out of hand and spread to the nearby woods. The men were arrested, and claimed before the judge to be members of a church whose teachings included instructions that the proper way to depart from earthly life was to do so by fasting. After fourteen days without food, the two had become too weak to keep their campfire under control and the fire spread. They spent the next thirty days in jail eating heartily. Another human-started fire resulted when a man and his children were fishing in an Idaho lake. Upon his children reporting that there were rattlesnakes in the nearby outhouse, he quickly poured gasoline down into the pit below the outhouse and tossed in a lighted match. Instead of burning, the gasoline and fumes from the accumulated wastes there exploded, sending the injured man to a hospital and igniting a small forest fire.

Fires have also been started by people looking for work. A fire warden in Washington State often arrived at a fire only to find local unemployed townspeople leaning on their shovels and waiting to be hired to put out the flames. The Rattlesnake Fire in California in 1953 was started by a man hoping to be hired by the fire crew as a cook. The fire ended tragically in the death of fifteen fire fighters.

Cupid also seems to have taken a toll on forests. During the 1930s one Civilian Conservation Corps

(CCC) crew in Oregon always seemed to be fighting fires on weekends. Fires would appear like clockwork as each weekend approached. It was later learned that local young men were displeased at having a CCC camp located near their town. The CCC members provided too much competition for the attentions of the local young ladies. The mysterious weekend fires kept the CCC crew members busy and the competition down.[9]

Strange fires seem to abound in California. A small fire broke out near a nudist colony. The sight of the smoke frightened the colony residents and they evacuated the camp for safety without bothering to claim their garments. The camp residents scattered into nearby woods. Word of the fire and details of the nudist evacuation were spread. Though it was not a big forest fire, at least 550 fire fighters reported for duty, along with the forest supervisor, regional forester, experimental station director, police chief, and the mayor.

An especially unusual fire ignition also took place in California. A forest-fire investigator pieced the story together from the remains of a snake. According to the investigator's hypothesis, a snake caught a small gopher and was in the process of swallowing it whole when a hawk swooped down on the snake for an easy meal. As the hawk tried to fly back to its perch with the twisting snake, the hawk lost its grip and dropped the snake. But instead of landing on the ground, the snake draped over two power lines and caused a short circuit. The snake was electrocuted and sparks dropping to the ground started a fire. When the fire was traced back to its starting point, the investigator spotted the charred remains of the snake still draped over the power lines, with a live gopher wriggling in its jaws.

1. Pyne, S. (1982), *Fire in America, A Cultural History of Wildland and Rural Fire*, Princeton University Press, p. 24. Or: Bell, R. (1899), *Forest Fire in Northern Canada*, Report of the American Forestry Congress, Washington, DC, p. 53.

2. Perry, D. G. (1987), *Wildland Firefighting—Fire Behavior, Tactics & Command*, Bellflower, CA: Fire Publications, Inc.
3. Morgan, C. (April 1988), "Wildfire!", *Reader's Digest*, v. 132n, p. 162.
4. deGolia, J. (1989), *Fire—The Story Behind a Force of Nature*, Las Vegas, NV: KC Publications, Inc., p. 8.
5. Perry, D. G. (1987), *Wildland Firefighting—Fire Behavior, Tactics & Command*, Bellflower, CA: Fire Publications, Inc.
6. Ibid., pp. 158–159.
7. National Wildfire Coordinating Group (1986), *Firefighters Guide*, Boise Interagency Fire Center, section 43.1.
8. Randall, C. E. (1969), "Crazy Blazes," *American Forests*, v. 75, n.8, pp. 8, 53–54.
9. Ibid., p. 166.

BATTLING BLAZES

SMOKEY THE BEAR

In 1944, a volunteer advertising council began a search for a national symbol for the forest-fire prevention effort. Poster campaigns using military themes, Bambi from the Walt Disney film, and scenes depicting devilish-looking forest fires were rejected. The prevention effort needed a unique symbol. Eventually, the council chose a bear. Early artwork featured a panda-style bear wearing jeans and a forest ranger campaign hat with a leather chin strap, and a face with a quizzical look. The bear symbol was named Smokey after "Smokey Joe" Martin, a fire fighter from the New York City Fire Department in the 1920s. Smokey the Bear got his voice from Washington, D. C., radio newscaster Jackson Weaver, who recorded his voice as he spoke into a wastebasket. Smokey the Bear was a hit with the public from radio commercials and appearances on posters across the country. Smokey reminded people to be careful with fire with the slogan "Only you can prevent forest fires."

Six years later, in 1950, a Forest Service helicopter pilot was flying over a burned-out section of the Lincoln National Forest in New Mexico. The pilot spotted an orphan bear cub on the ground. On landing, the cub was captured. It weighed only eight pounds and its fur was singed and its paws badly burned. First-aid treatment of the burns was administered at a fire camp near Capitan, New Mexico, and the cub was then flown to

Sante Fe for more thorough veterinary treatment. The cub was an unfriendly patient and tried to bite anything that moved.

The bear was at first nicknamed "Hotfoot Teddy" but someone later suggested the cub take on the identity of Smokey the Bear. Smokey the Bear cub was carried to Washington, D. C., in late June 1950 for a ceremony, and then given permanent residence at The National Zoological Park. Smokey was an extremely popular attraction and lived to the ripe old age of twenty-six before dying in his sleep in 1976. Smokey never produced an heir but in 1971 an abandoned, starving one-year-old bear cub was found in the same forest as Smokey. The cub was brought to the National Zoo to reside there as Smokey II.

FIRE PREVENTION

Well before Smokey the Bear urged people to be careful with fire, government agencies were engaged in fire prevention and control. In the early days of settlement of the country, fires were often ignored until they threatened property. Great fires in the 1800s were permitted to burn each summer without interference by landowners as long as the fires did not reach buildings and railroad lines. Organized U.S. Government efforts to control forest fires began with Army efforts to suppress fires in Yellowstone National Park in 1886. These efforts were followed by prevention policies that created organized campgrounds to contain fire hazards in relatively small areas.

A few years later some states, especially those with major lumber interests, began establishing forest preserves, organizing fire patrols, and appointing fire wardens. Railroad companies had an important stake in forest-fire protection because fire burns railroad ties and wooden trestle bridges. Sparks from railroad engines often ignited the fires in the first place and railroads aided in the fire-fighting effort by permitting rapid mobilization of fire-fighting crews to the fire scene.

In 1905, the state of Maine and the logging industry joined together to create a fire-tower lookout system linked to a central station by telephones. In the same year the Forest Service was created, within the Department of Agriculture. The job of running the Service was given to a friend of President Theodore Roosevelt, Gifford Pinchot. Trained in Europe as a forester, Pinchot applied the science of forestry to the lands the new agency was managing. Rather than the haphazard protection previously given to U.S. forests, Pinchot sought a coordinated program of research, production, and protection. Five years later he said:

In the early days of forest fires, they were considered simply and solely as acts of God, against which any opposition was hopeless and any attempt to control them not merely hopeless but childish. It was assumed that they came in the natural order of things, as inevitably as the seasons or the rising and setting of the Sun. Today we understand that forest fires are wholly within the control of man.[1]

Pinchot's philosophy, which set the direction of forest-fire control in the United States for the next sixty years, was based on his training in Europe, where forest fires were something to be prevented.

The year 1910 was a disaster year for U.S. forests. Summer fires in Idaho and Montana merged into huge uncontrollable fire complexes that eventually burned 5 million acres of land (7,800 square miles [12,536 square km]). The devastation left by those fires reinforced Pinchot's philosophy that all fires should be fought. Some

*An early fire tower, one of the first attempts
at an organized fire-fighting policy*

people, however, suggested a return to the Native American method of deliberate light burning at the right time, to eliminate accumulations of fuel and thereby reduce the possibility of major fires.

Fire research in the 1920s showed that coordinated, aggressive action by fire fighters while fires were still small generally kept them that way, and also kept the cost of fire-suppression efforts low. By 1935, the Forest Service established the "10 A.M. Policy" that called for all fires to be controlled by 10 A.M. the following day, before the hottest and driest part of the day began. This policy meant that fire fighters would have to rush to the fire as quickly as they could and throw everything they had at it to contain or put it out. Help for the 10 A.M. Policy came from the Depression of the 1930s. President Franklin D. Roosevelt established the Civilian Conservation Corps to provide outdoor work for unemployed young people. In 1933, one thousand CCC members were pressed into service in the great Tillamook fire in Oregon. After burning for ten days and covering 40,000 acres, the fire blew up and grew to more than 240,000 acres in less than a day. The fire storm that erupted reportedly had flames reaching as high as 1,600 feet (487 meters) into the air.[2] The CCC continued fire-fighting until 1942, when it was disbanded during World War II.

Though general Forest Service policy was to suppress fires, light burning experiments were conducted in the South as a possible aid to the softwood tree industry. Light burning cleared out slow-growing hardwood trees that choked out the more desirable pines. The southern experiments demonstrated that fires, under the right conditions, can actually help forests.

By the 1960s, fire policies across the United States were being changed to incorporate research pointing to the beneficial effects of some fires. Today, there are many agencies that administer forested land. These include

61

the Forest Service, National Park Service, Bureau of Land Management, Bureau of Indian Affairs, and state, county, and local forestry departments. Each have their own policies, which range from full suppression of all fires to suppressing some fires while letting others burn under carefully controlled conditions.

FIGHTING FIRES

Modern forest policies do not classify all forest fires as harmful. Although scorching forests and destroying trees, fires often lead to vigorous new growth and a diversification of animal and plant species.

Under natural-burn policies, fires are permitted to burn within certain limits. Fires must have been started by natural causes and they must fall within a prescription—that is, the fires and the general weather and geographic conditions have to meet certain criteria. Fires may be permitted to burn unless they threaten property or threaten to blow up into major conflagrations. Human-caused fires, except for those deliberately started for land-management purposes, are always suppressed. Fortunately, most forest fires burn out on their own and cause little damage. However, fires that fall outside the let-burn policy limits can be very destructive and must be fought from their start whenever possible.

TACTICS

Fighting forest fires is much like a military operation, except there isn't any shooting. Fire-fighter crews march out like platoons of infantry to battle a dangerous enemy. Using hand tools, they establish a fire line and dig in to hold the fire's advance. They may call in air strikes of water or chemical fire retardants to slow its spread. When the fire falters, the crews move in and mop up

*A fire fighter putting out hot spots
during the Yellowstone fires*

hot spots. Incident commanders, like generals, coordinate the efforts of the many crews and keep track of progress and the success of the effort.

FIRST LINE OF DEFENSE

The front line defense in any fire-suppression effort is the line crew—the men and women who do the dirty, backbreaking job of constructing fire lines. A *fire line* is a road or path-size line cleared of all unburned fuel ahead of the fire's advance. Its purpose is to stop the fire's advance by denying it new fuel. Using bulldozers, chain saws, or combination hand tools like the Pulaski—a two-sided tool consisting of an ax head and mattock at the end of a wooden handle—the line is cleared of all combustible material. Depending upon the rapidity of the flame's advance, the fire line may range from a few feet wide to a highway-size swath.

Upon arrival at the fire scene, the first task for the incident commander is to size up the fire. This has to be done quickly, before potential opportunities for controlling the fire are lost. The incident commander will consider fuels in the immediate path of the fire, slopes the fire can race up, the potential for spot fires, the weather, and natural barriers like roads or streams that can be used to assist in stopping the fire's advance. The incident commander will pay close attention to the time of day because midday fires have a tendency to flare up while nighttime fires tend to lie down. If the fire threatens to take off and race in a particular direction, the entire crew may have to be concentrated in one location while the incident commander radios for reinforcement and air strikes of fire retardants. Air temperature, winds, and relative humidity of the air are also considered. With all this information in hand, the incident commander can formulate a coordinated plan.

The attack on the fire begins. The fire fighters stretch

Fire fighters cut through dense
underbrush to form a fire line.

Heavy equipment is often used to clear the fire line.

out in a line across the fire's advance or completely circle it if the fire is small and on level ground and wind conditions are low. If the fire is moving quickly, a hasty line is constructed by clearing out the fastest-burning fuels and depositing them behind the planned fire line on the opposite side of the fire.

The line is improved by scraping the earth down to mineral soil. This is the sandy or clay-rich soil beneath the surface debris of leaves and needles and even beneath hummocky, organic-rich topsoil that can burn under the right conditions. A dug line may go even deeper than that because days or weeks after the fire is presumably put out, flames can emerge on the other side of the fire line from smoldering deep tree roots. If this situation is expected, the line should be cut through the roots as well. The soil dug up for the line is thrown on hot spots to cool them down and extinguish them. To work best, dirt must be shoveled onto glowing embers quickly before they have a chance to heat up again and continue burning.

Fire lines are best dug downslope from an advancing fire or on a ridgetop. A fire line dug upslope from an advancing fire has to be wider than a downslope line. Flames bend upslope as they move upward. The flames simply reach out and cross a narrow fire line to touch and ignite unburned fuels on the opposite side. Upslope lines are also more dangerous for the line crew because a change in the weather can set the fire running upslope faster than the crew can evacuate the area.

Whenever possible, natural fire breaks like lakes, barren ground, roads, and streams are taken advantage of to establish a complete defense. Roads and power-transmission line clear-cuts also form excellent breaks, although clear-cuts still have grass and scattered shrubs that can burn. These barriers minimize the possibility that the fire will flank around the dug fire line and menace the fire fighters from the rear. Furthermore, the natural barrier is an instant fire line that saves fire fighters

67

a lot of line-construction work. The line is started at the existing barrier and is moved across and parallel to the fire's path. The complete barrier combining fire lines and natural barriers is called a *control line.*

Proper placement of the fire line is important to the success of the fire effort. The first thought is to save as much of the forest as possible by beginning the line right next to the flaming front. But unless the fire is stalled and not moving forward, setting the line adjacent to the fire is counterproductive. A fire line is effective only if it is completely without gaps. Fires will burn around short fire-line segments, isolating the line from the rear and creating an island of unburned fuel, soon to be consumed, in the midst of the conflagration. To work, the line must form a complete barrier to the fire's advance. Even though more trees may be lost by constructing the line yards or even hundreds of yards ahead of the fire's advance, the extra distance from the fire will provide the necessary time to properly construct the fire line. The line will have a good chance of stopping the fire right there. With an incomplete line, however, fire can sweep right around and burn the trees that would have been cut for a proper line, plus many more.

Line width is important as well as line placement. Fire will simply leap over a line that is too narrow for the conditions. A line that is too wide takes too long to build and wastes time that could have been used to complete the line before the fire head reached it. Generally, a line should be as wide as one and one half times the height of the prominent fuels it is constructed through.[3] A fire racing through 8-foot-high (2½ meters) shrubs is likely to be stopped by a 12-foot-wide (3½ meters) fire line. If high winds are present, the line has to be much wider. Gale-force winds at Yellowstone in 1988 permitted fires to leap across half-mile-wide natural barriers, like the Grand Canyon of the Yellowstone.

BACKBURNS

Part of the strategy for containing fires behind fire lines may include the *backburn* technique. Once the fire line is completed, much unburned fuel may still lie between the fire line and the fire. The incident commander may judge that a backburn can be safely used to bring the fire to a speedy conclusion. A backburn fire is set to consume the remaining fuel, producing a very effective fire line made up of fire-fighter-constructed lines and scorched land. Backburn is a common fire-control technique but one that cannot be employed in all situations because it can "backfire"—the fire may travel the wrong way. Backburns, in essence, "fight fire with fire."

During many fires, convection currents, driven upward by the fire's heat, can modify local weather conditions to create a wind that is drawn inward to the burning area. The wind can be so strong that fire fighters need heavy jackets to shelter them from the cold air blast, even though a raging inferno is just a short distance away. The inward flowing air rapidly draws the backburn fire into the main fire. Eventually, the two fires meet somewhere in the middle and the fire head's advance is stopped.

The backburn is started by fire fighters who walk along the inner edge of the fire line igniting the unburned fuel inside the line with fusees (road flares) or with a special device called a drip torch that drips a flaming mixture of diesel and regular gasoline to the ground from a canister. Backburns are also set with flamethrowers and helitorches that are large versions of drip torches slung underneath helicopters.

When conditions are wrong for a backburn—erratic wind, too high humidity, improperly constructed fire line—backburns can backfire. This took place in the summer of 1988 outside the northeast corner of Yellowstone National Park near the towns of Silver Gate and Cooke City. On September 6 weather forecasts and predictions by fire-behavior specialists of increased activity of the Storm Creek fire led fire fighters to believe the two communities were threatened. The fire was expected to move into the Pebble Creek drainage and then through the canyon like a roaring blowtorch. A hasty fire line had been cut by felling trees with chain saws, but no opportunity was available to properly improve the line by clearing all fuel from it. Backburns have to be set at the right moment so that the backburn flames spread in the direction of the advancing fire. If fire fighters wait too long to set the backburn, the fire head will get too close and not allow enough time for the backburn to consume the fuel in between. The two fires will mass together and keep advancing in the wrong direction. Troublesome winds defeated the Storm Creek fire backburn by rolling flames over the fire line and by sending flaming debris through the air to start spot fires. The fire proceeded past Silver Gate to within 50 feet (15 meters) of Cooke City. Four cabins were lost to the flames. Angry residents claimed the backburn was unnecessary. Fire officials countered that given the same conditions and the same information they had to work with, they would still have set the backburn. They fully believed the advance of the Storm Creek fire would have affected every home in the valley. Furthermore, most fire damage, they said, was caused by spotting and not the backburn itself.[4]

MOP-UP AND CONTROL

The goal of fire fighting is to extinguish fires, but this requires much more than constructing fire lines and backburning. As long as there is fire anywhere in the burn area, there is danger of a flare-up. Fires thought to be out have been known to flare up from smoldering wood weeks later when the weather changed. *Control* means keeping the fire within the line.

When a fire has been contained, one of the legs of the fire triangle has been nearly eliminated—fuel. The fire is deprived of new fuel and will probably go out. But "going out" could take months if the weather is right. More effort is needed before fire fighters can move on. The *mop-up* phase of the fire-suppression effort begins. This is the dirtiest and the most tedious job. Mop-up crews walk into the burn area near the control line and literally turn over every charred log to search for hot spots. How far they walk into the burn from the fire line depends upon the potential for the fire to flare up again. They feel for heat by holding the backs of their hands over logs and piles of white ash. When hot spots are found, they are chopped open or dug up and doused with water to cool. Water is sprinkled on, and the ground is stirred to make sure the water gets to where it is needed. In the absence of water or as an added effort, the mop-up crew will shovel dirt to cool and deprive hotspots of oxygen. Even roots have to be dug up to look for glowing embers. Still-standing trees, *snags,* may have to be felled, especially if they are flaming or glowing.

FIRE CREW

Since World War II, there has been a movement toward mechanizing fire-fighting efforts with heavy equipment like bulldozers and air tankers to achieve cost-effective control of wildfires. Although one bulldozer can do the work of many fire fighters in constructing fire lines, hand crews are still the backbone of any fire-suppression effort. The effect of mechanization is to supplement and not replace the hand crews.

The initial attack is usually the domain of the fire fighter. In all fire-suppression efforts, time is the principal factor in a successful suppression. The sooner suppression efforts begin, the more likely the fire will be stopped before it can do much damage. *Smoke-chaser teams, helitack teams,* and *smoke jumpers* are the quickest and most efficient way of beginning the attack on most fires. Smoke chasers arrive on foot, carrying the tools they will need in packs. A smoke chaser team is small, often just two fire fighters. One serves as the incident commander and makes decisions of where and how to best get the job done. If roads lead into the fire area, the team may be followed and supplemented by fire engines and bulldozers.

Helitack teams and smoke jumpers are employed especially when it is a long haul over rugged terrain to the fire. Brought by helicopter or cargo aircraft like a DC-3, fire fighters can often be on the scene less than an hour after the fire is sighted. Helitack teams arrive by helicopter. If clear ground is available for a safe landing, the helicopter discharges a crew of a half dozen or more fire fighters, depending on load capacity. If the ground is not clear, fire fighters can rappel down ropes as the helicopter hovers and then, using hand tools, open a *helispot,* a small clearing of trees and shrubs for a helicopter landing site. Repeated trips of the helicopter bring in supplies and hand-crew reinforcements.

The fastest response to a distant fire, when ground wind conditions are right, is by the elite smoke-jumper crews. Smoke jumpers ride cargo planes to the fire scene and bail out. On the first pass over the fire, the spotter, in the cargo section, sizes up the situation by tossing out colored streamers to mark the direction of wind drift. If the streamer drops down in the desired landing site, the jump is made from the same point on the next pass. If not, the plane goes around again and more streamers are tossed out farther upwind. The idea is the smoke jumpers' drop will follow that of the streamers.

Wearing protective clothing, including football helmets with heavy wire face screens, smoke jumpers jump into clearings if they are lucky, into brush, and even into tall forests where their parachutes may get hung

*Smoke jumper crews parachuting in to
fight a fire in Glacier National Park*

up on treetops. They may have to jump out over the fire in order to drift to where they want to be. The air blast as they leap out the side cargo door is fierce and often slaps them onto their backs. The chute is pulled by a static line attached to the plane, and a sudden pop and jerk assures them their parachute is properly deployed. Pulling down on control lines opens panels on their parachute canopies to dump air from one side and get some action/reaction thrust so they can have some steering capability.

Padded smoke-jumper jumpsuits have thick, high collars to protect their heads from tree branches as they attempt to "slide" through the treetops on their way down. If hung up, they can descend on ropes or climb down the branches after they release themselves from their parachutes. On additional passes of the cargo plane, tools, food, sleeping bags, and water are dropped by cargo chutes.

On the ground, smoke jumpers fight fires with hand tools and construct fire lines. If the fire is too big for the smoke-jumper crew to handle, their efforts become a holding action until reinforcements and heavy equipment arrive to relieve them. They then head back to a road for a truck or car pickup and return to their smoke-jumper base so they can be ready for the next assignment. Heading back may mean hiking out with 110 pounds of equipment on their backs.

Big fires, or those that are expected to get big, and those near communities, require more fire fighters. Hotshot crews, consisting of nineteen tough, well-trained fire fighters, may be brought in. Each of the dozens of hotshot crews across the United States are organized into three squads of six members each, with one member serving as a squad boss, and a crew boss. Hotshot crews are forest fire versions of the military rapid deployment force. They travel from one large fire to another and assume the dirty, backbreaking work of fire line construction, setting backburns, and doing mop-up. When forests across the United States are ablaze, hotshot crews will establish fire lines and may then be replaced by less-trained crews who assume the job of holding the line and later mop-up of the fire site.

Fire fighters on the line are only part of the fire-suppression effort. Many people provide a continuing flow of supplies, coordinate activities of fire crews, plot and predict the fire's progress, monitor the weather, call in air strikes of fire retardants, and survey the damage so that, if desired, the land can be rehabilitated with tree seedlings and any bulldozer and other fire-suppression scars can be repaired. The total effort is not just the private domain of the professionals. Much outside support is also needed. During the 1988 Yellowstone fires, for example, local restaurants were contracted to cater food for the thousands of hungry fire fighters returning to fire camps at the end of their shifts. Local motels were used as billets for some of the fire-fighting crews. Millions of dollars were spent in the Greater Yellowstone Area to take care of regular fire fighters and the soldiers brought in for reinforcements.

TOOLS OF THE TRADE

The fire fighter's basic tool kit for constructing fire lines and for mopping up consists of many items. Although high-tech devices have been created for battling blazes, hand tools are still the staples. Fire fighting is hard, grungy work and the best tools are variations of agricultural hand tools that have been used for centuries. In use are single and double-bit (blade) axes, shovels, mattocks and hoes, and rakes. Since fire fighters often have to carry all the gear they need to do their jobs on their backs over rough country and carry it back afterward, packing equipment is not a happy task. To make things easier, a couple of special combination tools have been created by fire fighters themselves (and carry the inventor's name) so that one tool can do several jobs. A Pulaski is a versatile tool that combines the best features of an ax and a hoe at the head of a single wooden handle. The hoe side of the head is for breaking and overturning soil to create a fire line. It can also be used for turning over smoldering logs to allow application of dirt to smother embers. The ax is for cutting down trees and brush. Another fire fighter–invented tool is the McLeod. The McLeod combines the features of a hoe for soil-breaking with a rake for gathering smaller-diameter fuels to deposit them across the fire line.

In addition to the basic fire-fighter hand tool kit for small operations, there is also power equipment for bigger efforts: chain saws to quickly cut down trees; pumper fire engines, called *ground tankers,* that carry water in tanks or can draw water up from lakes and streams to wet down burning material with sprays from fire hoses. If the terrain is too rough for fire engines, pumps holding about five gallons of water are carried by fire fighters on their backs. Pumping motions with a two-handed nozzle, something like a home garden sprayer, directs water streams onto burning material. Fusee (road flares) torches, drip torches, and flame-throwers are used for setting back fires. Then there are personal items like knapsacks for carrying clothing, food, and first-aid supplies, and hard hats, gloves, and fire-resistant clothing and boots. Also carried are compasses and maps, electric head lamps, portable fire shelters, sleeping bags, and canteens. Crew bosses and incident commanders carry radios to keep in touch and weather monitoring equipment to keep track of any changes that could lead to dangerous conditions.

AERIAL ATTACK

During the height of the 1988 Yellowstone fire season, the fire-fighting team in the Greater Yellowstone area assembled an air force that was larger than that of many countries.[5] When the call went out for help, fixed wing and rotary wing (helicopter) aircraft converged on the area from all over the nation. Aircraft were used for transporting fire fighters and supplies, and in direct assaults on the fires.

During the fire-suppression effort, thousands of water and fire retardant drops were made. The principle is simple. The fire is doused with water, a water-and-foam combination, or a magenta-colored mixture of water, fertilizer, gum, and red dye to cool flaming fuels and put them out, or at least cool them to give fire fighters on the ground time to build their fire lines.

The idea of assaulting fires from the air was first attempted during experiments conducted in the Soviet Union. About the same time, in the United States, the fire chief in the Spokane, Washington, region experimented with aerial fire control by kicking out 5-gallon beer kegs filled with water from an old Ford Trimotor aircraft.[6] The barrels burst on impact with the ground but their spread was limited because so little water was involved. In a second experiment, water was also sprayed out of nozzles from the same aircraft. The spray was totally ineffective because it vaporized before it hit the ground. Nevertheless, the experiments were first steps toward a major technological leap in wildfire fighting.

Beer kegs were replaced by actual bombs with proximity fuses set to burst the bombs just over the ground. These were rejected in favor of bombs that burst on impact with the ground, kicking up dirt and mud which added to the extinguishing effect.[7]

The first operational fire retardant bombing on a fire did not take place until 1950. Development of aerial techniques was delayed by World War II. Paper bags lined with latex rubber and filled with water were dropped from a DeHavilland Beaver and achieved effective results.[8] Paper bags were later replaced by rotating 50-gallon water tanks, and then by tanks inside the bellies of aircraft and in pontoons.

Aerial bombing today is done by large tankers, such as a C-119 or a C-130, which can hold up to 3,000 gallons of water and retardants.[9] Flying just a few hundred feet above the flaming treetops, they discharge their loads by opening from one to eight doors or gates to release varying amounts of water. Water or retardant mixtures spread out, covering swaths of land. A *salvo* (several or all doors at once) from a C-119 can cover an area of 90 by 750 feet (27 by 229 meters). Single-door openings in sequence can stretch the wetted area on the ground to several thousand feet while narrowing the width to the range of 10 feet (3 meters). This is called a *trail drop*.[10] Salvos are especially effective for use in direct control on small fires and spot fires. These fires are simply blasted with water from above. Salvos are also good for use in surface fire control, where dense tree canopies of leaves act like umbrellas. Massive drops ram through the canopies to the surface. Trail drops are used as a delaying effort to cool fire heads and give fire crews time to construct fire lines.[11]

Most fixed-wing aircraft in use today for fire fighting are cargo aircraft modified with water tank and drop systems. Canada, however, has a large fleet of aircraft specially built for fire control. The CL-215 waterbomber aircraft looks like a large seaplane with pontoons on the wings. Rather than returning to a land base for refills, it swoops down on large lakes like an eagle about to snag a fish swimming on the surface. Scoops protruding from beneath the belly of the CL-215 suck in 1,410 gallons of water in just ten seconds as the plane skims the lake.[12] If the fire is near a lake, as it often is in many parts of Canada, the CL-215 can average ten drops an hour from altitudes as low as 75 feet. A more powerful version of the CL-215 will be able to deliver 36,000 gallons on a fire in just eight hours of opera-

Dropping a load of 7,000 gallons of water
at a time, this Canadian plane fills its tanks
from a lake close to the fire it's fighting.

tion. As a bonus, a foaming kit is installed that injects chemicals into the water as they are dropped. The foam expands eight to twelve times in volume, causing the water to nearly double the size of its drop area and increasing its effectiveness by 25 percent.[13]

Canada developed the CL-215 because of its wide expanses of forest and lakes. Searching for fire outbreaks there is now done primarily by air, eliminating the need for hundreds of lookout towers, and the waterbombers are used for holding actions until ground crews can arrive.

Helicopters make excellent aerial bombers because they can hover and make precise drops if needed. Large fabric helibuckets are slung by a cable beneath helicopters and dipped into lakes to take on a load of water or to lift loads of retardants from portable mixing tanks where water and fire-retardant chemicals are blended. Unlike waterbombers, helicopters can use small lakes and even ponds as a water supply. Water or retardant loads are smaller than tanker loads. Large, military helicopters can hold up to 700 gallons of water.[14]

During the Yellowstone fires, aerial bombers and helicopters dropped 1.4 million gallons of fire retardant on fires, and helicopters alone dropped 10 million gallons of water.[15] In spite of erratic high winds and persistent widespread smoke that made flying difficult, the safety record was excellent. The only fire-related aerial accident took place when a helicopter crashed while refilling a helibucket with water to dump on a fire. The pilot recovered fully from the crash.

"SHAKE AND BAKE"

Fire fighters develop a healthy respect for nature. Though they may brag about putting out a fire by their own efforts, they freely admit that forest-fire fighting is usually a matter of maintaining a holding action to keep the fire from spreading excessively until the weather improves or the fire simply runs out of fuel. When conditions change for the worse, forest fires quickly let fire fighters know who is boss. A blowup can consume tens of thousands of acres in an hour and send flames racing through the woods faster than a fire fighter can run. Exhausting efforts to build fire lines to hold the advancing blaze may be wasted by fires that flank the line and come around behind the fire crew. Fires spotted by firebrands at the rear of the fire line may grow and merge and cut off fire crew escape routes. Often, the land the fire is raging on is too rugged for anything but a slow retreat. In this condition fire fighters may be trapped and killed as fire sweeps over them.

The Butte fire in Idaho's Wallace Creek drainage in the Salmon National Forest[16] demonstrates how dangerous forest fire fighting can be. On August 29, 1985, a 118-person fire crew was working feverishly to improve a 50-foot-wide bulldozer-cut fire line that had been set the day before. The crew boss hoped the line—cleared of all flammable debris left after the bulldozer's efforts—would permit a safe backfire to be set, so fuel could be burned off and the approaching fire stopped. Their efforts were a race against time, with everything stacked against them. The Wallace Creek area was ready for a blowup. The land was dry and each acre contained an estimated 90 tons of fuel ready to flame.

The improved bulldozer line ran along a ridgetop. At 2 P.M., the fire, 2 miles (3 kilometers) below, began gaining in intensity. What had been a nearly stalled, slow-creeping fire quickly changed into a "tidal wave of flame" that raced upslope toward the crew. The crew's only hopes for survival rested on special four-pound tents, carried in yellow pouches on each fire fighter's belt. Referred to flippantly as "brown and serve" bags or "turkey roasters," the pup tents seemed unlikely to be able to provide shelter from the 30-story-high wall of flame advancing on them.

Crew bosses directed everyone to retreat to 350-foot-wide (107 meters) circular safety zones that had been cut by bulldozers at quarter-mile intervals along the line. The 118 fire fighters divided into two of the zones, with 73 fire fighters in a zone directly in the path of the approaching maelstrom of flame. The crew boss gave the command "deploy shelters." The crews rephrased the order as "shake and bake" time. Each fire fighter quickly cleared a 4-by-8-foot (1 by 2 meter) rectangle of land of flammable materials and unfolded a shelter. The tents, properly called *fire shelters,* are made from a thin layer of aluminum foil laminated to fiberglass cloth with a nontoxic adhesive.[17] The foil is designed to reflect away 95 percent of the flame's radiant heat. Only 5 percent of the heat is absorbed and enters the tent. The shelter gradually gets warmer and temperatures can reach over 150 degrees Fahrenheit (66 degrees Celsius) inside, but even prolonged exposures to such temperatures is survivable. Dry saunas often reach 190 degrees Fahrenheit (88 degrees Celsius).[18]

The two layers of material are shaped as a floorless pup tent with diagonal straps in each corner. The pup-tent shape permits the fire fighter to lie flat against the ground with his face pressed to the dirt to find the coolest and cleanest air. The shelter's low profile keeps it fairly stable even during high-buffeting winds.[19]

The roar of the flames pounded the 73 fire fighters in the middle of the safety zone. Winds of 70 mph (113 kph) buffeted the shelters, threatening to send some airborne. Inside each, the fire fighters, though terrified, held their ground bravely. Their arms and legs were spread-eagled to press down on the corner straps to hold down the shelters. Through pinholes, they could see the light outside change from red to orange to white as the fire's full fury fell on them. The air inside was stifling but breathable. Air as hot as 500 degrees Fahrenheit (260 degrees Celsius) can be breathed safely for a short time providing it is very dry and breathing is shallow.[20] The fire fighters shouted to each other and exchanged stories to keep up their courage and to assure each that others were still alive.

The blaze abated for a time but then returned from a different direction. The fire fighters crawled turtlelike inside their shelters to distance themselves from the front. Finally, an hour and a half after entering the fire shelters, the fire moved away from the safety zones and the fire fighters could emerge from their shelters. All were alive and, except for some cases of dehydration and heat exhaustion, no one was seriously hurt. Meanwhile, outside the shelters, shovels and other tools dropped nearby had been reduced to metal blades. The wooden handles had burned completely away!

HIGH-TECH FIRE DETECTION

In the early days of forest fire fighting, fires were detected by sight and smell. Someone would spot a cloud of smoke or a nighttime glow in the sky in a direction where it didn't belong. Or favorable winds would drive smoke from a fire many miles from the backcountry to a village, farm, or ranch where someone would smell it. Later, organized networks of fire towers were erected in forested areas and staffed daily by people whose job was to look for "smokes." With the advent of the airplane, smoke spotters look to the air. Still later, as we entered the space age, satellites were employed to map large fires in remote areas.

Today, all the past methods plus a few high-tech new ones are in use. The concept behind their use is straightforward. The sooner a forest fire can be detected, the better it can be dealt with. If the fire is going to be put out, a small fire is much easier and cheaper to extinguish than a big one. If the fire is going to be permitted to burn, accurate and up-to-date monitoring is essential to keep the fire from getting out of hand.

One of the oldest techniques, seeking the high view, is still the most effective for forest-fire detection. Forest-fire towers in the New England area were the first to allow an over-the-tree look at the countryside. Tower operators spent their days and sometimes nights looking for smoke or flames. Using a compasslike device, they would take a sighting on the fire, and telephone or radio its position to a fire dispatcher. On a large map in the dispatcher's office a line from the tower's position would be extended in the compass direction reported. When reports came in from other fire towers, additional lines would be drawn, and the location of the fire could be determined from their intersection points.

This fire-detection method is still widely employed and was important to the fire effort in the Greater Yellowstone Area in 1988. The compasslike device used for fixing on fires is the *Osbourn Firefinder*. The Firefinder is mounted on a tabletop in the middle of the windowed house at the top of the tower, and leveled so that in addition to compass directions of fires, an approximate determination of their elevations can also be made. A pair of hairline sites on opposite sides of a circular map, representing the view from the tower, slide around the map on a movable ring. When the fire is aligned in the two sites, the compass angle is measured at the base of the ring. A sliding peephole site nearest the operator's eye is moved up and down until a cross hair on the opposite site is exactly aligned. This provides an angle measurement for the rough determination of the fire's elevation up high ridges.

Airplane surveillance of forested areas is an especially effective way of spotting fires in areas too remote for a network of fire towers. In the United States, aircraft were first employed in forest-fire detection patrols around Puget Sound in Washington State in 1915. A few years later, airplanes were given the additional job of airlifting supplies to fire camps. In the mid-1930s, planes were even used to take pictures of large fires. The film was developed by on-board darkrooms and dropped to fire fighters as an aid to planning attack strategy. Unfortunately, airplanes today are expensive to operate and are still limited by weather and by range. During fire seasons, the airplanes are needed to assist ground fire crews by reporting on fire spread and spotting activity of large fires. There may not be enough planes to go around to keep watch for new fires.

Satellites seem like an ideal way of looking for new fires and monitoring existing ones. But, like airplanes, satellites can be affected by weather. Satellites with instruments to collect images from reflected light are blocked by clouds. Smoke from big fires may be blown over large regions and can mask the smoke from newly started fires. However, satellites with infrared sensors can pick out small fires through clouds and smoke. Another problem with satellites is that if they are in low orbits, they are over each forest for only a few minutes at a time and, depending upon the orbit, it can be more than a week before the satellite passes over again. A hefty lightning storm can start many new fires before its return. Satellites in high geostationary orbits (orbits in which satellites remain over the same geographic point on the Earth's equator) provide continuous views, but at a distance of 22,300 miles (36,000 km), detail in the images they send down is of limited value for early fire detection. Only the largest fires can be picked out easily. Nevertheless, satellites are useful, especially in long-term studies of the fire environment and studies of the recovery of an area after a fire.

Short-term aerial fire monitoring is a useful method

for plotting the progress of fires but it is hampered by slow data processing. Aircraft flying from 10,000 to 50,000 feet (12,045 meters) above the blaze can photograph it, but the film has to be dropped to the ground, developed, and used by human mapmakers to plot the fire perimeter on topographic maps. A completed fire perimeter map can take as many as six hours to complete, which is an acceptable time if the fire is slow-moving. However, if the fire is racing, it can progress as much as 10 miles (16 km) during that time, making the map useless.

To remedy the time problem, the Forest Service is working with scientists and technicians at NASA's Jet Propulsion Laboratory in California to produce almost "real time," or immediate, fire-perimeter maps. In the planned system, an aircraft will fly overhead with an on-board infrared scanner to measure radiation from the fire. The data it collects will be radioed to a receiver on the ground where a computer will be used to store and process the data. A plotting machine (mechanical drawing device) will draw the fire perimeter directly on a topographic map of the area. The finished product will be ready in about twenty minutes. An advanced satellite system may someday provide updated images every thirty seconds. In addition, the system could help researchers evaluate the effectiveness of fire-suppression strategies. For example, the effectiveness in slowing a fire's head with a fire-retardant drop would be seen easily.

The computer age has brought a number of new high-tech tools to aid in fire detection. Satellites—though still limited in real-time visual observations—are now playing an important part in the prediction of dangerous fire conditions. The West is now dotted with hundreds of automatic solar-powered weather stations where wind speed and direction and air humidity are sampled, along with temperature and the moisture and temperature of soil, brush, and timber. The information gathered by these unmanned stations (called RAWS, for remote automated weather stations) is relayed by passing overhead satellites to a central location where computers and their human operators analyze fire hazard conditions. The data they assemble tells them where lightning strikes or careless human use of fire are likely to trigger wildfires. With this information, fire-fighting crews can be alerted to a state of readiness and be provided with information about potential trouble areas.

Quicker detection of lightning-started fires, leading to faster deployment of fire-fighting resources, has reduced the average size of these fires to less than one acre.[21] A network of 40-foot-high (12 meters) antennas has been constructed in the West to serve as *direction finders* for lightning detection. Mounted on valley floors to avoid electrical interference sources, the direction finders send pulses of digital data to a computer at the Boise (Idaho) Interagency Fire Center each time lightning strikes within the 225-mile (363 km) range of the tower. Like a "dagger," lightning strikes from cloud to ground cut through the air and produce a wave of electromagnetic energy that radiates in all directions like "dropping a rock in a pond."[22] Direction finders detect that energy and send digitized signals to the computer. With two or more direction-finder reports, the computer, like a fire dispatcher with fixes from Osbourn Firefinders, fixes the location of the stroke.

During heavy storm activity, tens of thousands of lightning strokes will be recorded and mapped by the computer. Copies of the maps are sent to regional forest offices. The maps, combined with RAWS data, are useful in setting the flight paths of spotter planes that will go out to check if a fire has actually started. Instead of being sent to fly in huge grid patterns to cover the entire region, the planes are sent to the area of greatest lightning activity. According to Ken Reninger of the U.S. Bureau of Land Management: "We used to fly planes around everywhere just looking for a fire. It was like jumping in a taxi and saying: 'Take me someplace.' Now we can go directly to where the lightning hit."[23]

It is unlikely that high technology will ever replace the fire fighter who battles a blaze with hand tools. But high technology—lightning detectors, RAWS, computers, pocket calculators programmed to enable fire-line crew bosses to predict fire behavior while they are fighting fires—is providing information to make fire fighters' efforts on the ground more effective, less expensive, and less dangerous.

THE GREAT PESHTIGO FIRE OF 1871

The famous Chicago fire said to have been started by Mrs. O'Leary's cow when its tail knocked over a kerosene lantern into a pile of straw was a mere shadow of a fire when compared to a fire that was raging at the same time several hundred miles to the north in Wisconsin. The summer and fall of 1871 in northern Wisconsin had been especially dry. From the beginning of July through October, no rain fell—a very unusual occurrence. The ground became parched. Wells, swamps, and streams dried. Standing vegetation, fallen leaves, and underbrush "became so dry as to be ignitable almost as powder [gunpowder], and ground itself, especially in the cases of alluvial or bottom lands, was so utterly parched as to permit of being burned to the depth of a foot or more."[24]

Scattered fires raged through northeastern Wisconsin from the centrally located Horricon Marsh, which was on fire itself, to the shores of Lake Michigan. Farmers, lumberers, and railroad workers were all called upon to protect property. Since wells had run dry, they resorted to ringing sawmills, homes, railroad lines and wooden trestles, and other structures with ditches to serve as fire lines. As long as there were no strong winds, the ditches would hold. By early October, long-hoped-for rains did not come and among the exhausted fire fighters and other residents a "general gloom and fear seemed to have come upon the threatened region."[25]

In the forests and in cities and villages such as Green Bay, Appleton, Menomonee, and Kewaunee, the smoke was so dense that travel from place to place was difficult and the danger of getting lost always present. Fire had spread so close to the railroad lines that trains had to run at full speed whenever possible to avoid catching on fire. In some instances, trains had to chance running across burning wooden trestle bridges to escape advancing flames. People sought refuge from the flames by excavating small tunnels and covering their entrances with earth. Dry wells were also used as refuges. Some property owners sought to protect their furniture and household possessions by placing them in the middle of cleared fields. Ironically, the protected furniture was often destroyed while the homes were spared. On Saturday, October 7, the exhausted people felt they could take a breath. Although rain had not come, the fires had burned over everything that could be burned, and people thought they could begin rebuilding. The worst was over, they thought.

But the next day, Sunday, October 8, saw no letup to the fires. They became worse. In the village of Sugar Bush, residents heard an "unusual and strangely ominous sound, a gradual roaring and rumbling approached. It has been likened to the approach of a railroad train—to the roar of a waterfall—to the sound of a battle, with artillery, going on at a distance. The people, worn out with the long, harassing fire for weeks before, quailed at this new feature, and when the flames did make their appearance—not along the ground, as they had been accustomed to meet them, but consuming the treetops and filling the air with a whirlwind of flame—the stoutest hearts quailed before it."[26] The fire had returned as a fire storm of swirling flames. Pine treetops were twisted off and flung by the gale-force winds, and debris was sucked up from the ground to be set on fire. "The smoke was suffocating and blinding, the roar of the tempest deafening, the atmosphere scorching, children were separated from their parents and were trampled upon by the crazed beasts (horses, oxen, cows, dogs, swine); husbands and wives were calling wildly for each other and rushing in wild dismay, they knew not where. While others, believing that the day of judgment was surely come, fell upon the ground and abandoned themselves to its terrors."[27] In minutes Sugar Bush was burned away completely.

In Peshtigo, Wisconsin, the same fire storm wiped out virtually the entire town. Peshtigo, a sawmill city, was located on the banks of a river in which some of the city's 2,000 inhabitants sought refuge. Some of them drowned outright in the river, or were trampled on by panicked horses, cows, and swine driven into the river by the flames. A great number of people sought refuge in a wooden boardinghouse and all perished as flames rendered it to a pile of ashes and cinders. Others died when the flames caught them in the open. Many more were suffocated by smoke or their breathing passages were burned by the hot air. Some jumped into dry wells, but even these provided no safety.

The fire storm proceeded toward the great bay between Wisconsin's mainland and the peninsula and then up into the peninsula itself. A steamboat captain who had remained at shore in the midst of a shower of sparks and firebrands, took on a cargo of terrified victims and steamed out into the bay to safety. All across the peninsula panicked people sought desperately to save themselves. As many as fifty people tried to cram into a shallow pit, not six feet across, that had been used for storing potatoes. Others sought refuge in wells and shallow, dry streambeds. Some survived by moving into tree stands that earlier had been completely burned over. Abbé Pernin, a Catholic missionary living at Marionette later wrote of the fire:

It was a grand spectacle to observe this fire in the night. It shot up to the summit of the largest trees, the flames coiling around them like immense serpents, and leaping from branch to branch, they illuminated the whole country. Darting tongues of fire into the midst of the green foliage, they created a moaning and roaring through the forests as in a fearful tempest.[28]

The Great Peshtigo Fire of 1871 was the worst forest-fire disaster ever in the United States. It burned out more from a lack of fuel and changes in the weather than any other reason. Thousands of square miles of forest lands were burned, and though an accurate count could never be made, it is believed that at least 1,500 people died in the flames or while attempting to escape.

---

1. de Golia, J. (1989), *Fire—The Story Behind a Force of Nature*, Las Vegas, NV: KC Publications, Inc., p. 18.

2. Ibid., p. 19.

3. Perry, D. G. (1987), *Wildland Firefighting—Fire Behavior, Tactics & Command*, Bellflower, CA: Fire Publications, Inc., p. 273.

4. Simpson, R. W. (1988), "The Fires of '88, Yellowstone Park & Montana in Flames," *American Geographic Publishing Montana Magazine*, pp. 46–49.

5. Cone, P. (1989), *Flying*, v. 116, n.1, pp. 55–56.

6. Linkewich, A. (1972) *Air Attack on Forest Fires, History and Techniques*, Calgary, Alberta: D. W. Friesen and Sons, Ltd., p. 35.

7. Ibid., p. 35.

8. Ibid., p. 34.

9. Perry, D. G. (1987), *Wildland Firefighting—Fire Behavior, Tactics & Command*, Bellflower, CA: Fire Publications, Inc., p. 221.

10. Pyne, S. J. (1984), *Introduction to Wildland Fire—Fire Management in the United States*, New York: John Wiley & Sons, pp. 386–387.

11. Ibid., p. 386.

12. (1989), "Turbine Engines Will Improve CL-215's Fire-Fighting Capability," *Aviation Week and Space Technology,* v. 131, n. 8, p. 50.
13. Ibid., p. 42.
14. Ibid., p. 217.
15. "The Greater Yellowstone Fires of 1988—Questions and Answers" (news media fact sheet provided by the park management at Yellowstone National Park), p. 3.
16. Turbak, G. (1986), "To Hell and Back in a Pup Tent," *American Forests,* v. 92, n. 9, pp. 29–31, 46–48.
17. USDA (1986), *Your Fire Shelter,* Forest Service Equipment Center, p. 2.
18. Ibid., p. 2.
19. Ibid., p. 1.
20. Turbak, G. (1986), "To Hell and Back in a Pup Tent," *American Forests,* v. 92, n. 9, p. 48.
21. Nieman, S. (1985), "Wired Forests" *American Forests,* v. 91, n. 6, p. 31.
22. Ibid, p. 31.
23. Witkin, G. (1986), "Fighting Forest Fires the High-tech Way," *U.S. News & World Report,* v. 100, n. 25, p. 58.
24. Robinson, C. D. (1872), "Account of the Great Peshtigo Fire of 1871," reprinted in Hough, *Report on Forestry,* p. 231.
25. Ibid., p. 232.
26. Ibid., p. 233.
27. Ibid., pp. 233–234.
28. Ibid., p. 237.

FIRE ECOLOGY

Ecology is a specialized branch of biology that studies living things in the context of their environment. It was developed because biologists realized that it is not possible to gain a complete understanding of a living organism just by looking at it as though it were a specimen in a bottle. A field mouse, for example, can be looked at as a living package of flesh, bones, and organs, but this view covers only a small part of what a field mouse is. It is a strand in a complex of living and nonliving things and forces called an ecosystem. The mouse lives because it gets energy from seeds and nuts provided by plants. It breathes in oxygen purified by plants, and exhales carbon dioxide that plants then take in to produce glucose through the light-energy-driven process of photosynthesis. It drinks water recycled through the atmosphere. The mouse's waste products provide nutrients needed by other living things, and the mouse itself becomes food for predators such as owls and hawks. The field mouse's habits are dictated by climate, seasons, and day/night cycles, and it modifies its environment by digging burrows for its home.

Each other living thing in the field mouse's environment is also a complex body of interactions. When each known interaction is plotted on a piece of paper, lines linking different living and nonliving things become an intricate "web of life."

Until the last few decades, one important strand in the web was often disregarded: the strand of fire as a great eraser of old growth and a recycler of nutrients. "Fire is a profound biological event."[1] Where it is prevalent, it alters the living environment by cleaning out forests of accumulated fuels and of invading and less desirable plants. It encourages new growth and diversification of plant and animal species, and it releases nutrients accumulated from sunlight, minerals, and water and locked-in dead material for use in new growth. Fire drives off pests, parasites, and diseases. It opens the forest floor to sunlight and promotes berry-bearing plants favored by birds and other wildlife and thereby encourages their abundance. It creates prairie lands by burning off trees. Fire prepares forest soil for new growth and may turn it into an exceptionally rich seedbed.

Fire and living things have a kind of symbiotic relationship—each needs the other. Fire requires fuel provided by living things in order to burn, and living things require fire to rejuvenate. Many organisms, especially plants, have developed significant defenses against fire while others have evolved adaptations that actually promote fire.

Adaptation to fire depends upon the *fire interval* or the frequency with which fire affects an ecosystem. Fire makes its appearance in different environments at different frequencies. Natural fire is virtually unknown in tropical rain forest regions. Although the climate is generally very hot and there are often intense and violent electrical storms and lightning strikes, fire rarely gains a foothold because of the high humidity in rain forests and the high moisture content of rain forest fuels. When living things die, the nutrients in their tissues are readily released through the active decomposition (rotting) that takes place in a warm climate and humidity.

In more temperate climates, fire is a common factor, in some areas occurring every decade or so. Growth rate of new vegetation in temperate regions normally exceeds the rate of decomposition of dead material. Without fire, soil eventually becomes depleted of its nutrients. Fire is essential to release these tied-up nutrients for new growth.

In cold, dry climates, growth and decay are slow. Fuel takes longer to accumulate. Small fires occur frequently but their effect on the total region is negligible. However, every 100 to 200 or even 400 years, fuel accumulates to such an extent that major fires are inevitable. In a large, sweeping episode of flame, the forest is given a "jump start" back to an earlier stage in its succession (the stages in which different plants and animals invade an area).

Fire is a necessary and inevitable part of many ecosystems. The longer an area goes without fire, the greater the accumulation of fuel—leaf and needle litter, dead branches, and weathered and diseased and pest-infected standing trees. The greater the accumulation of fuel, the more likely fire will occur. Furthermore, the greater the accumulation of fuel, the hotter the fire will be, the more rapidly it will develop, and the more likely it will spread widely.

WHAT IS FIRE ECOLOGY?

Fire ecology is a branch of ecology that concentrates on the origin of fire and its relationship to the living and nonliving environment. Fire ecology recognizes that fire, though appearing infrequently, "has been a natural part of ecosystems since the origin of climate on earth."[2] Fire was around long before human beings arrived to become a source of and a suppressor of fire. Vigorous forests and grasslands existed in relationship with fire for eons without human intervention. Ecologists know that understanding of an ecosystem requires more than just observing it as it is. An understanding also requires knowledge of how the ecosystem came to be, what it may become, and how it cycles through its various stages. Fire is one of those stages.

FIRE INTERVALS

The question can be asked, "How do we know what the fire interval—the time between successive fires—of a forest is, especially if it is a very long interval?" The answer is that the trees themselves tell us through their annual growth. A tree that has been charred by fire but not killed will preserve fire scars in its interior wood as it continues to grow. Trees heal by growing over scars and other damage to their trunks. Anyone familiar with old farmsteads will probably remember seeing trees that were used to support barbed-wire fences. The living tree "posts" continued to grow and expand after the barbed wire was attached, and enveloped the wire into their bark and the wood itself. When the tree is cut down, a rough estimate of when the wire was attached to the tree can be made by counting the number of tree rings that have grown past it. Each ring represents the growth of one year. The same holds true for fire scars. The year when a fire occurred can be estimated by counting rings inward from the current year's ring just beneath the bark, to the ring where the fire scar is located. Samples of different trees throughout a region may even indicate the extent of the fire spread by the locations of trees touched by a particular fire.

Multiple fire scars enveloped by tree growth can provide an indication of the fire interval of a particular area. A 100-year-old tree with four fire scars more or less evenly spaced through its rings points to occurrence of fire on the average of every 25 years. Many of the ancient trees of the West, like the Douglas fir *(Pseudotsuga menziesii)*, have dozens of scars to tell their fire story. Trees without fire scars also tell a story. A stand of 200-year-old trees with no fire scars would indicate a fire interval of more than 200 years. Tree stands with trees all approximately the same age indicate a major tree-stand-clearing fire wiped the land clear of trees and gave the current trees in the stand a chance to begin growth about the same time.

In addition to fire interval data, tree rings also provide climatic data. In wet years, tree rings grow thick and in dry years they remain thin. Often, several very thin tree rings precede a scar from a major fire episode, indicating several years of drought leading up to the season when fire occurred. This information can be compared to current climatic data and may provide some indication of how big future fires, should they occur, might be.

Living trees are not the only source of information on fire intervals. *Fusain* is fossilized charcoal that was created during an ancient forest fire. In Yellowstone National Park, some of the fossilized trees have fossil fire scars indicating that fire has been a natural part of the Yellowstone environment for ages.

Studies of the fire interval of the Yellowstone region indicate more than one interval exists in the park. Trees in portions of the park's northern range experience fire on the average of every 25 years. Lodgepole pines in the great forests of the park's interior experience the more typical fire interval of 250 to 400 years. Interval studies indicate that the park region is studded with frequent small fires but these are "interrupted by occasional years of extreme climate conditions that allow huge areas to burn. One such fire event occurred in the early 1700s and another in the mid-1800s."[3]

SOIL AND WATER CHANGES

Virtually every fragment of an ecosystem is touched in some manner when fire occurs. The effects from low-intensity burns can be minimal and those from high-intensity burns are profound. In essence, fire can be good or bad for an ecosystem depending on when and where it takes place and on its magnitude. Fire can alter soil to make it more productive or bake it to the point of sterilization so that nothing can grow in it for a time.

Soil is made up of a mixture of mineral and organic particles. Organic particles from decaying vegetative matter perform valuable service to a forest or any other land ecosystem. Organic matter helps break up soil minerals like clay to permit rain and snow melt-off to infiltrate to the lower soil zones where plant roots grow. The surface layer of needle and leaf litter helps to moderate soil temperatures so that soil neither gets too hot in summer nor freezes too deeply in winter and thus damages roots. Litter reduces soil moisture evaporation and also disperses the impact of heavy raindrops to cut erosion damage. But the effects of organic matter at the surface varies by the amounts. Too little matter can promote erosion. Too much can dry the soil because it can absorb as much as one-half the water in a heavy rain and nearly 100 percent of the water in light showers.[4] Following the rain, most of the absorbed water never seeps down to the soil but is lost to evaporation and contributes to the drying of a forest floor.

How fire affects forest soil depends upon the fire's intensity and duration. A low-intensity burn will clear out centuries of accumulated litter to release nutrients leading to improvements in the soil that will encourage seed germination. A high-intensity burn can bake the soil and break down organic components, driving certain released compounds downward to form a hydrophobic or nonwettable layer, in other words, a layer that repels water. This soil-damaging condition leads to increased water runoff and erosion and retards the growth of seedlings. Fortunately, the conditions under which a damaging hydrophobic layer forms are limited. Soils that are dry and sandy are more susceptible than fine-textured wet soils to hydrophobic layer formation. Examination of the Yellowstone soils has revealed that the principle change in the majority of burned areas was a surface charring. Just beneath the charred layer were a multitude of still living and flexible plant roots, indicating that heat did not penetrate the soil very deeply. Estimates of soil heating in Yellowstone National Park indicate that only about 1 percent of the soil received heating extreme enough to produce a significant hydrophobic layer.

Fire removal of soil organic material also creates important changes in food supplies—in numbers of forest-floor animals and of plants living in soil. Healthy, organic-rich soil hosts a virtual menagerie of microorganisms, insects, and small vertebrate animals. Inhabiting the soil are insect larva, mites, termites, spiders, ants, centipedes, millipedes, beetles, snails, nematodes, earthworms, mice, moles, and many other tiny creatures. Plants of the organic soil litter include algae, fungi, and lichens. Each of these living things exists in and on the shallow organic layer. When fire comes, the layer is changed dramatically from the perspective of these small organisms. Fire reduces the numbers of organisms by three to tenfold and it takes as many as five years for them to reestablish themselves.[5]

The damage to the upper layers of soil can lead to significant soil-erosion problems the next spring. Snow melt-off, combined with spring rain, can wash away upper layers down to mineral soil in a matter of days or even hours depending upon soil slope. Steeply sloped banks are subject to rapid runoff and heavy erosion, while gentle slopes retard runoff erosion. Slopes are measured in percents. A 10-percent slope drops 10 feet (three meters) vertically for every 100 feet (30 meters) of horizontal distance. Research has shown that if surface litter cover is reduced by half, erosion rates increase dramatically. Studies in western Montana revealed that the water runoff from snowmelt was eight times greater on burned-over areas where the vegeta-

Soil erosion as a result of a forest fire

tive cover was reduced by 50 percent compared to control areas where the cover was 98 percent intact.[6]

If there is time before the winter snows set in, fire rehab (rehabilitation) crews may begin work on burned critical slope areas to establish erosion controls. Downed trees are anchored across slopes to act as water runoff dams to slow flowing water and recapture sediment. Late-season grasses and tree seedlings are planted as soil anchors. Plastic mesh may be spread over the ground as well to minimize erosion. Soils that are lost, especially those in a high-altitude northern zone where the soil formation rate is very slow, can take hundreds if not thousands of years to replace.

With water runoff comes problems with water quality in streams, rivers, and lakes. Since fires can cook soil, leading to increased water repellency, water runoff is increased. Turbidity, or muddiness of the water, and sedimentation from the soil carried in runoff water can damage water quality and aquatic organisms in a number of ways. Increased sedimentation may silt in bottom-dwelling life, cutting it off from sunlight and even the exchange of oxygen with the water. Food supplies for fish will temporarily diminish. Fish-spawning areas are harmed by sedimentation. Furthermore, more rapid soil runoff will increase the velocity of rivers and streams, making it difficult for fish to spawn in the first place and washing out spawning beds. The mineral and organic quality will change, raising the alkalinity of the water, affecting aquatic life used to other conditions.

The damage fire causes to waterways is not limited to runoff problems. Trees falling into a river can clog it, causing the force of running water to be diverted which, in turn, affects riverbank erosion. Fallen trees produce barriers to fish migration. On the other hand, fallen trees can also create pools for improved fish habitat. If riverbanks are cleared of living trees, the water will no longer be shaded from sunlight part of the day;

seasonal river temperatures may rise to higher than normal levels, which may lead to increased fish and bottom-life mortality. However, at higher elevations, the reverse can be true. Lack of shade can raise water temperature earlier in spring, encouraging a longer growing season for plants and aquatic life.

The Greater Yellowstone region was fortunate in the spring of 1989. The general warming trend leading to summer was much more gradual than usual, slowing down the snow-melting rate. Instead of quick melt-offs, snow meltwater had more time than usual to seep into the soil. This minimized soil-erosion damage and damage to the region's water resources.

RESPONSES OF SELECTED LIVING THINGS TO FIRE

Coastal Redwood and Giant Sequoia

Every living thing, plant or animal, that exists in an environment touched by fire has its own response to or strategy to deal with fire. Individual responses tell a remarkable story of adaptation. Some living things, like the giant redwood trees of California, have evolved strategies that permit them to stand fast, endure fire, and continue growing. A walk through a coastal redwood *(Sequoia sempervirens)* forest reveals many healthy trees standing more than 200 feet (60 meters) tall yet repeatedly scarred at their bases by fire. Coastal redwoods respond to fire through thick fire-resistant bark that permits the tree to survive low-intensity surface fires. Fire leaves scars and where it penetrates to the wood a wound is started that is slowly attacked by rot. More fire comes and works on the wound, widening it. Eventually, through rot and successive fire, cavities large enough to pitch a tent in are formed at the base of many coastal redwood trees. Yet, between bark and charred wood is healthy, living, and growing wood.

Although coastal redwoods do not necessarily depend on fire for survival, fire does prepare the soil to serve as a seedbed for redwood germination. Fire also kills off Douglas fir seedlings and young trees that often grow in close proximity to the redwoods. Douglas fir trees can act as fire ladders to carry flames to the tops of redwood trees, killing them off. Long periods without fire permit the shade-tolerant Douglas fir seedlings to climb to the growing tops of redwoods. Short fire intervals retard Douglas fir development. Fire also clears and opens the redwood forest floor to prepare a better seedbed and encourage the growth of food-producing plants for wildlife.

The giant sequoia *(Sequoiadendron giganteum)* reaches a more massive size than the coastal redwoods and is found inland on the slopes of the Sierra Nevada mountains of central California. Rather than resisting fire, the giant sequoia depends upon late summer fires for survival. Scientific studies of experimental plots of giant sequoia and control plots convincingly demonstrate the tree's fire dependence. Experimental plots that have been purposely burned are profusely covered with as many as 22,000 giant sequoia seedlings per acre. Control plots that have been protected from fire are often completely devoid of seedlings.[7] Fire clears out the growth of other plants that cover the forest floor and inhibit the growth of the giant sequoia seedlings that are needed to replace old trees as they die.

Fire scars on the giant sequoias point to the frequent incidence of fires in their domain. The scars are generally found on the lower trunks of the trees, indicating that crown fire is relatively rare. In thickets where fire has been suppressed by human beings, shade tolerant white fir *(Abies concolor)* trees have grown to the base

103

of the sequoia crowns, creating a critical fire situation. White firs make excellent fire ladder trees. Again, frequent fire reduces competing species growth while sparing the dominant trees.

In clearing out surface fuels, fire also performs another important function for the giant sequoias. The seeds of this giant tree are small and produce short roots that quickly deplete the seed's nutrient supply. If seeds fall on forest litter, the chances are poor that the roots will ever reach the soil before the nutrients run out. Fire clears out the litter and makes a good ash bed for quick germination of the seeds. Soon the forest floor is covered with a green carpet of sequoia seedlings.

Giant sequoias have also evolved another significant fire adaptation that is shared by a number of tree species. Its cones are serotinous. This means that the cones remain closed long after the seeds inside are capable of germinating. Heat from fires triggers the opening mechanism of the cone so that seeds are dropped to the ground after the fire has passed. This form of seed distribution leads to explosive reproduction of new seedlings.

Chaparral

In California, fire makes a frequent appearance. The brushlands and scrubby forests of chamise, scrub oak, manzanita, and other evergreen plants are collectively called chaparral. Chaparral vegetation areas are about the most fire-prone wildlands in the United States. Fires, often speeded along by the dry and hot Santa Ana winds, move with frightening velocity and violence. Fire suppression costs and losses to homes and other property can easily exceed $50 million annually.

Chaparral vegetation is a bundle of good and bad. On the positive side it is essential for soil stabilization on the steep slopes found throughout California and is well-adapted to drought, poor soils, and frequent drying winds. Chaparral vegetation provides food and habitat for rabbits, deer, bobcats, rodents, and many species of birds. It further provides browse for domestic grazing animals. On the negative side, chaparral vegetation is highly prone to fire. On its own, this is not necessarily bad. However, many chaparral ecosystems have been altered by the spread of urban development. The quest for new human habitation areas has led to the placement of many thousands of homes directly in the midst of the chaparral. When wildfire strikes, much more than vegetation is at stake. Property and human life are at risk as well.

Chaparral vegetation is highly adapted to fire and it actually promotes fire by the way it grows. Many varieties of chaparral vegetation contain large amounts of oils, resins, terpenes, and waxes in their stems and leaves. The proportion of these highly flammable chemicals increases during the fall dry season as moisture content drops, leading to a dangerous situation. The extractives lower the ignition temperature of the plants so that fire is more easily started and may spread more rapidly.

Another fire-promoting adaptation of chaparral vegetation is a growth pattern that favors many smaller stems over a single large trunk. With smaller diameter stems, the temperature of the vegetation is more easily raised to ignition point. The arrangement of the stems and twigs places them just close enough together to quickly spread fire while permitting fresh oxygen to enter to sustain burning. Furthermore, chaparral has a tendency to accumulate dead branches that continue to remain standing for many years. In two or three decades, chaparral may reach a 50–50 ratio of living to dead wood. This creates a hazardous fire condition year-round.

Fire clears off chaparral vegetation from the surface

but rarely damages root systems. The chamise has specialized buds in its root crown. Sometimes, less than two weeks following a fire, these buds grow to become new stems that reestablish the plant. By retaining a living root system even after a fire, the chamise and similar plants continue anchoring the soil to prevent severe erosion and soil loss. Other chaparral shrubs produce hardy seeds that can lie dormant in the soil for many years until heating alters their hard shells and permits them to germinate. Still more amazing are some annual broadleaf herbs that are unable to germinate because of the chemical action of certain soil microorganisms. The fire destroys the chemicals that permit the annuals to bloom in abundance for a few seasons. When the microorganisms reestablish the soil chemicals the annuals die off, but by this time many evergreens have returned.

Lodgepole Pine Forest

Lodgepole pine *(Pinus contorta)* is a tree species that grows widely throughout the western United States, running northward as far as the Yukon Territory in Canada. It can be found from sea level to nearly 12,000 feet (3,650 meters) of elevation in the central Rocky Mountains. A highly adaptable species, it can grow in a wide variety of soils, including those that are poorly drained and gravelly soils that are well drained.

The lodgepole pine forest presents an interesting study in fire ecology. In the Greater Yellowstone Area the different fire intervals range anywhere from 25 to 400 years. Because of the northern latitude, the climate is cool and the humidity is generally low. The soils are derived relatively recently from glaciers that retreated from the area approximately 12,000 years ago. The growth rate in such a climate is slow, and so is the decomposition rate of dead matter. At the time of the Yellowstone fires, about 80 percent of the forests consisted of stands of lodgepole pine that matured more than 100 years ago. Under this circumstance, heavy fuel loads can build up and lead to intensive fires with long flame lengths and rapid spreading rates. A 1987 report on the Greater Yellowstone Area found that of its 12 million acres, more than 50 percent had the potential for high-intensity fires.[8]

Each time a major fire sweeps through, a new succession begins. The growth of new plants begins immediately following the burn and animals quickly reinvade the area. When water is available, green shoots of the light-loving lodgepole pines begin to appear in a few days. If the land is dry, the bulbs and rhizomes that survived the fire's heat in the soil just beneath the surface and seeds from cones may wait until the following spring to sprout. In spring, the land explodes in color with grasses, wild flowers, and lodgepole pine and spruce seedlings. The new grass in particular provides forage for grazing animals. The only place devoid of growing things is the ground under and near fallen trees where the wood burned and smoldered many hours after the main fire passed, cooking and sterilizing the soil.

In just a few years, numerous other ground plants, including snowberry, dogbane, Oregon grape, and spirea reestablish themselves from living stems just beneath the soil's surface. Wild currant and snowbush germinate from seeds dropped and covered in the soil as much as thirty to fifty years earlier. Other plants return to the area through colonization. Dandelion and fireweed have fuzzy parachutes that permit them to be lofted by the breeze and dropped on the fertile soil. Some other colonizing plants "hitchhike" on animals by attaching themselves with tiny barbs and hooks to fall to the ground later as the animals graze in the abundant forage.

Lodgepole pines have serotinous cones that require heat to open and distribute their seeds. The heat melts and burns away resins that have sealed the cones and dries them out so that they open. Lodgepole pines also produce cones that open on their own and drop their seeds yearly. In tree stands where fire is a frequent visitor, the dominant cone type is serotinous. The seeds in nonserotinous cones would be destroyed. However, in old stands where the fire interval is very long, there is a shift to nonserotinous cones because the trees cannot depend upon fire to trigger seed release, and nonserotinous cone seeding assures replacement seedlings to fill in for trees that die.

Following the 1988 Yellowstone fires, representative seed sample counts were made in burned-out lodgepole stands. After the fires had passed, serotinous cones released their seeds along with nonserotinous cones that had survived the fire. Seed densities averaged between one and 20 seeds per square foot, amounting to 50,000 to 1,000,000 seeds per acre. Seeds that are not eaten by hungry mice, squirrels, and birds and that fall upon suitable soil survive to grow. Depending upon the condition of the soil at the spot they land on and the competition they receive from grasses and shrubs, there may be as many as a thousand new lodgepole pines an acre five years after the fire.[9]

As the lodgepole pines become established and begin intertwining their branches to close off the canopy, the lower branches die from lack of light and are shed. Should a fire come through the area again, it is likely to be a surface fire with no way to climb up into the canopy. As the soil beneath the trees is shaded, trees such as the subalpine fir, which has no resistance to fire, may invade through seeds transported in from mature nearby stands untouched by fire. Subalpine fir germinates best in shady conditions. As the trees mature, they can tolerate full sun and will grow to top out over lodgepole pines. This doesn't happen everywhere lodgepole pines grow. However, where it does, subalpine firs can create a fire ladder situation. If fire does not sweep through again to clean out the subalpine firs while still small, later fires, which will inevitably come, will wipe out both kinds of trees.

Animals

Many of us have a picture in mind from the old Walt Disney animated movie classic *Bambi*. Late in the movie a forest fire is carelessly started and the flames race through the woods. Panicked animals scatter in all directions as tongues of flame lash out, threatening to destroy them. It is an exciting and frightening scene but fortunately for real-life animals, it usually doesn't happen that way. Except when a fire blows up to become a crown fire, or is heavily fanned by gale-force winds, fire moves slowly enough through woods and across grassy and brushy areas for most large animals to escape. Wisps of smoke alert animals to a potential danger, and smaller animals, like rodents, seek shelter in their burrows and in rocky areas, or make a dash for the open in advance of the fire head. If the fire doesn't last too long and there is a sufficient supply of fresh air in their burrows, they survive. Otherwise, they succumb to smoke inhalation. Birds take to wing, and since it is rare for fire to come early in the breeding season, nests of fledglings are not threatened. Usually, the babies have grown sufficiently to take care of themselves.

As the 1988 Yellowstone fire season wore on, evening television newscoverage gradually shifted from the "horrors" of the flames to the fires' impact on wildlife, perhaps due to a growing realization by the news teams that forest life went on in spite of the flames. Newscasts began featuring wildlife stories. While fire fighters struggled with the flames in the background, bison and elk were shown, seemingly unperturbed and not at all panic-stricken, on the flaming edge of grasslands, grazing as usual. Backlit by flames, elk were seen and heard in their fall bugling rituals. Though the ground was still hot, elk were even shown stepping over flaming logs to

109

A bull elk grazes in Yellowstone near an area destroyed by fire.

get at patches of unburned browse in the midst of ash-covered land.

Like plants, many animals have their own fire adaptations. Grazing and predator animals are often drawn to fires to forage for food. Squirrels, chipmunks, and birds are drawn to the seeds dropped to the ground following the fire-induced serotinous cone opening. Predators have an easier time getting at rodents when fire clears off vegetation, and leaves few above-ground hiding places. The rare three-toed and black-backed woodpeckers are drawn to burned forests because the dead but still erect trees attract beetles. The woodpeckers have a feast and move on to another newly burned forest only when the forest they are feeding in rejuvenates itself.

Insects are probably the most affected animal life-forms during fires, which seems fitting because some varieties of insects strongly contribute to preparing trees for fire in the first place. Insects, like pine beetles, bore through tree bark and into the tree's trunk and branches, weakening the trees and making them more susceptible to disease infection. Infected trees are more easily burned than healthy trees. Fire beetles actually seek out fire. They apparently have sensors that are sensitive to infrared radiation and can detect fires as much as 60 to 100 miles (97 to 161 km) away. They arrive at the fire site to breed and the females lay their fertilized eggs in charred wood.

One resourceful bird species in Australia actually starts its own fires. The firehawk is a predator and will fly into a fire and pick up a smoldering twig and drop it in an unburned grassy area. The new fire drives out rodents and reptiles to make easy hunting for the firehawk and other birds.[10]

During the Yellowstone fires, wildlife biologists observed a raptor "feeding frenzy." Peregrine and prairie falcons, all sorts of hawks, gray owls, and eagles were actively hunting the fire fronts in open meadows as small

111

rodents like the vole, field mouse, and pocket gopher were driven from their burrows by the flames. It was as though the huge columns of fire and smoke sounded a dinner bell calling resident and migratory raptors into the area. More than forty ferruginous hawks, rare in the Yellowstone region, showed up for dinner in September perhaps attracted by the smoke.[11]

Scavengers, like bear, coyotes, and carrion birds, are attracted to fire to eat the carcasses of larger animals killed by the fires. During and after the Yellowstone fires, wildlife biologists kept close watch on the fires' effect on animals. Of great concern was the question of fire mortality on the ungulate populations—elk, moose, mule deer, and bison—and on the black and grizzly bear population. Surveys on fire-related animal mortality were conducted on the ground and by helicopter. Researchers discovered 335 elk, 12 moose, 36 mule deer, 9 bison, and 6 black bear carcasses in the fire zones within and outside the park boundaries.[12] On-site autopsies revealed that virtually all the animals probably died from smoke inhalation rather than from flames. This was determined from smoke deposits found in the animals' tracheas or windpipes. An additional moose and a black bear had to be destroyed outside the park boundary because they had been severely burned. No grizzly bear carcasses were found. More elk probably died in the fires but researchers chose to avoid two additional planned study areas because of extensive grizzly scavenging activities going on there. Just about all the carcasses were found in areas that had been swept by rapidly moving fires that allowed few avenues of escape. Few ungulates were found where fires had narrow or slow-moving fronts. All animal carcasses were left in place as meals for scavenging ravens, coyotes, golden and bald eagles, and bears.

Although elk, the most numerous ungulate at Yellowstone, accounted for most of the ungulate deaths in the Yellowstone fires, the known dead comprised only about 1 percent of the average elk population in the park at any one time. Of greater concern than the immediate fire danger to animals was the alteration of habitat. In Yellowstone National Park, approximately 50 percent of the winter elk ranges burned and extensive summer elk range burning also took place. Following the fires, many elk returned to their summer ranges, but an early migration to the winter range took place as well. Researchers believe the migration was due more to the summer drought conditions than to the fire that reduced browse quantity even where fires did not spread. The reduction in winter range and the harsh winter that followed led to at least 5,000 elk winter kills—a higher number than usual. Fire-induced habitat change also affects species of birds, like the sage thrasher and Williamson's sapsucker, which prefer old-growth habitat. They are likely to decline for several years following fires.

In the long term, wildlife habitat benefits from fires. In the following spring, grassland and marshy areas explode in lush new growth. Forests become a vigorously growing vegetative patchwork of trees in different stages of growth, providing habitat for many different kinds of wildlife. Nutrient-starved forest soils are recharged. Studies of plant and animal changes following fires indicate that there is often a threefold increase in both plant and animal species that reinhabit burn zones. However, after twenty-five or so years, the number of species diminish as the growing trees begin closing off the canopy overhead and shading the earth beneath, ultimately leading to another fire episode.

1. Pyne, S. J. (1984), *Introduction to Wildland Fire—Fire Management in the United States*, New York: John Wiley & Sons, p. 34.

2. Wright, H. A., and Bailey, A. W. (1982), *Fire Ecology—United States and Southern Canada*, New York: John Wiley & Sons, p. 3.

3. Schullery, P. (1989), "Yellowstone's Fire Regime," paper supplied by the National Park Service, pp. 1 and 2.

4. Wright, H. A., and Bailey, A. W. (1982), *Fire Ecology—United States and Southern Canada*. New York: John Wiley & Sons, p. 25.
5. Ibid., p. 31.
6. Ibid., p. 39.
7. Ibid., p. 358.
8. Simpson, R. W. (1988), "The Fires of '88, Yellowstone Park & Montana in Flames," *American Geographic Publishing Montana Magazine*, p. 33.
9. National Park Service (1989), *Yellowstone Fires 1988* (supplement to the *Yellowstone Today* newspaper), p. 3.
10. de Golia, J. (1989), *Fire—The Story Behind a Force of Nature*, Las Vegas, NV: KC Publications, Inc., p. 31.
11. National Park Service and USDA Forest Service (1989), *The Greater Yellowstone Postfire Assessment*, p. 81.
12. Ibid., p. 71.

5   CONTROVERSY

One of the inevitable by-products of a major forest fire is heat; not just the heat associated with flames but also the heat of controversy. Why wasn't the fire put out sooner? Who is at fault? Who will pay for the damage to property? Why weren't the fire crews better prepared? Who came up with this strange "let-burn" policy?

There is no doubt that a major forest fire is a catastrophic event that touches more than just the ecology of a forest. Human lives are altered. Big fires destroy homes, injure and kill people, and alter the local economy. Major tourist resorts and resort towns, even if missed by the flames, can be wiped out economically if tourists go somewhere else to more scenic, unburned areas.

Forest fires ignite controversy. Are fires ecological boons or disasters? Should fires be permitted to burn or be suppressed with every ounce of resource at hand? Whose interests are more important and should be protected? The battlefield of forest-fire controversy is filled with diverse interests. What do each of the opponents say? The opinions that follow here show what many different people said about the 1988 Yellowstone fires, in books, news stories, or in interviews. Their remarks are placed in the setting of an imagined public hearing on the 1988 Yellowstone fires and what should be done about future forest fires. Viewpoints of various groups are each presented by a representative. Statements and

115

ideas are taken from a number of sources. Some are exact quotes from real people and the person's name follows in parentheses. The source of each quote is indicated in footnotes. It is important to note that a person quoted in an ecologist's testimony, for example, is not necessarily an ecologist. Rather, the remarks are quoted because they are the kinds of concerns an ecologist would state.

PUBLIC NOTICE

Meeting Tonight at 8:00 P.M.

in the

Town Hall

Topic: FOREST FIRES: ECOLOGICAL BOONS OR DISASTERS?
Questions to be discussed:
• Were the 1988 fires in the Greater Yellowstone Region handled correctly by the National Park Service and the Forest Service?
• Should the "let-burn" policy be abandoned?

Greater Yellowstone
Area Resident
I'm mad as hell. My family and I moved up here because of the beauty of the region. Last summer's fires destroyed that. I have heard what the ecologists and the park rangers said about rejuvenation of the forest, but that is small consolation to someone who has to look out a living room window at what was once a lush green forest and now sees a blackened, charred cemetery full of tree skeletons. Sure, "everybody's working their buns off to get things back, but there's no way they can recoup. The park's going to be a black forest for a hundred years." (Trevor Povah)[1] "Our na-

tional heritage is burning down . . . to let it burn is a total outrage." (Ana May Kline)[2] People at park headquarters should have anticipated the 1988 fires and done something about it before it was too late. What do we pay them for—to sit around in their Smokey the Bear hats and smoke pipes?

Forester

I work for the Forest Service. It is a multifaceted agency of the federal government. We manage, protect, and promote U.S. national forests to meet a wide range of needs and expectations. My many years of forest experience has led me to conclude that under certain conditions, fire can be beneficial to many forest environments, and even absolutely required in some. Fire can be a powerful forest management tool if used properly. But uncontrolled fire is nearly always destructive. Fires, like the Yellowstone fires of 1988, produce dramatic changes in forests and it is a tragedy when large areas of trees are burned away. Many of the beneficial properties of fires can be derived from well-planned logging operations. Some logged trees, like the coastal redwoods, spring up with a profusion of new shoots, from the remaining stumps, that will grow into tall, strong new trees. The big differences between logging and wildfire is that through logging, wood does not go to waste and the skies are not filled with choking smoke. However, I am not suggesting we permit logging of the park, but I am suggesting that fire can be useful if it is not permitted to run out of control. Fires benefit forests by releasing nutrients tied up in old tree growth, to be used for new growth.

Ecologist

During last season's fires and in the many months that followed, many news and magazine reports spoke of the fire's effect on rejuvenation of the forest. Let me assure you, as a fire ecologist with many years of experience, that is exactly what happens. I wish I could say that the forest will return to its old self in just a few years. That is just not so. What has happened is that the forest has cleaned house. Where crown fires swept through the Yellowstone forests, old and diseased trees were wiped out. Their days were numbered. If not fire, something else would have gotten them first, but they would have burned inevitably. Some of the most distressing forest-fire aftermath pictures that were published were of tracts of land where all the charred trees were squashed to the ground. The pictures emphasized the fire's destruction. In fact, those pictures showed old, disease-weakened lodgepole stands that were blown over and killed by high winds several years before. As much as we would have it the other way, trees are not forever. They start from seed, grow tall, and ultimately die. Fire is one of nature's ways of clearing out the old to make way for the new.

Rather than killing the forest, last season's fires have given the forest floor a big dose of tonic. Nutrients long locked up in the old trees have been released and the light-blocking forest canopy has been opened, permitting direct sunlight to reach the soil. This spring, we saw a carnival of color—greens, yellows, blues, violets, and reds—from the explosion of new growth of wild flowers, grasses, shrubs, and tree seedlings. Accompanying new growth has been a rapid increase in the populations and kinds of insects and larger animals seeking the abundant new food supplies.

Everyone here tonight is interested in protecting Yellowstone. Without factual knowledge of how the entire ecosystem, including fire, functions, we are just laboring in the dark.

Business
The fires were a disaster for local business. Sure, we were able to do business with the fire fighters and that

helped to make up for some of the loss in tourist dollars, but we are scared as hell of the long-term effects of the fire on our business. I don't buy park bosses' statements saying they "didn't know it was a dry year." That's hogwash. Every farmer in this region knew, yet these so-called naturalists and inflexible bureaucrats went ahead with their 'let 'er burn' policy—picking the driest year in fifty years to experiment with a national treasure. We think it's an unmitigated disaster." (David Flitner)[3] It is a good thing the park bosses have the backing of the federal government. If we ran our businesses the way they ran Yellowstone, we would be closing our doors within the week.

Fire Fighter

I'm a fire fighter and for "the past twenty-eight years I've been both fire boss and a grunt digging line with a Pulaski. I've fought, taught, set, and investigated fires. But I've not seen a fire season like this past one." (Donald Wood)[4] Nothing in my experience prepared me or my fellow fire fighters for last summer's fury. It was like opening a new book. So much was unexpected. "Fire amounting to a flicker at daybreak erupted to a thousand acres by nightfall. Some fires known to exist could not be found because of the heavy smoke." (Wood)[5] I vividly remember August 20. People now call that day "Black Saturday." More than 150,000 acres went up in flames. I think that "every professional fireperson saw things that none of them had seen before in their lives. People who had been fighting fires for thirty years were just in awe." (John Varley)[6]

I have heard many people complain that the Park Service waited too long to start fighting the fires and that is the reason the fires were able to run out of control. Sure, the early fires were permitted to burn at first, but by mid-July, all fires were being suppressed. Up to that point, only about 20,000 acres had burned. The really big North Fork fire was suppressed right from the beginning. "We threw everything at that fire from Day One. We tried everything we could think of, and that fire kicked our ass from one end of the park to the other." (Denny Bungaraz)[7] In spite of all our best efforts that fire eventually covered more than a half million acres.

People generally have a mistaken idea about forest fire fighting. We fire fighters come out with our engines, helicopters, tankers, bulldozers, and hundreds of line fighters swing Pulaskis and McLeods and give the impression that we are in control. At best, all we do is speed up the natural fire-extinguishing process that will happen on its own at any rate. "In a typical fire season, fire fighters do not generally stop a fire until Mother Nature lets them do so: the winds die down, evening coolness and dew help out, or maybe a shower comes by. Last year nothing helped—the winds kept up, no moisture came, the temperature stayed high." (Wood)[8]

The let-burn policy in Yellowstone is a good policy. It succeeded for fifteen years before 1988 came along. We still have much to learn about natural fires. Let-burn is a "good and useful tool in the forestry kit. The wise craftsman doesn't blame his tool when a job gets out of hand—he learns to use it more proficiently. We must not eliminate the let-burn device—we must learn to use it better." (Wood)[9]

Tourist
My family and I came to Yellowstone last summer on vacation. We had expected to see bears and geysers but were not prepared for the show of our lives. The fires were unbelievable and terrifying to watch even from a distance. The smoke filled our lungs and stung our eyes constantly while we were here.

Why did the fires have to burn like that? Places that we had visited here during an earlier vacation were incinerated. We have heard that the park bosses have some dumb idea that fires should be allowed to burn here. Perhaps fires should be permitted to burn in wilderness areas that most people never see but not in Yellowstone. This is the people's park and I think it was a tragedy and maybe even a criminal act to let the fires grow so that they ran out of control. If I had screwed up as badly in my job as the people we trusted our park to did in theirs, I would have been fired on the spot.

Environmentalist

I applaud the efforts of the Park Service in attempting to permit the natural course of events to take place in Yellowstone. We have been cutting down, plowing up, pushing over, dumping, polluting, littering, and in general fouling the environment for decades. Then we stand back like crybabies and yell at the Park Service for not controlling a natural process. We're lucky to have any natural processes left. Fire suppression is unnatural and that is part of the reason the fires were so big last year. If you force the forest to build up flammable fuels by not letting periodic small burns take place, and if you don't do something to manually clear out the fuels, the inevitable happens. We got what we deserved. "This is a part of the ongoing evolution of the greater Yellowstone ecosystem. I personally haven't encountered a scientist who thought that this represents devastation and that it's something terrible that shouldn't have happened." (James Schmitt)[10] The fires will help Yellowstone return to its natural state.

Park Ranger

I know that I am speaking for my fellow park rangers when I say that we are as sincerely interested in protecting Yellowstone as anyone else here tonight. Serving in the park is not just a job for us. We love

Yellowstone and will continue devoting our professional lives to it.

I resent remarks by people who characterize us as do-nothing idiots who let a national heritage go up in smoke. I also do not like to hear of park policies that permit natural fires to burn under carefully monitored conditions described as "let-burn." Let-burn implies that we sit around the fire toasting marshmallows as trees are destroyed. Let-burn *doesn't* mean do nothing. When forest smokes rise from lightning strikes or a visitor is careless with fire, we are on it (the fire) as fast as humanly possible. If it is a human-made fire, we give it every bit of effort we've got to put it out. If the fire is natural, we monitor it and the weather closely to make sure it follows our prescription. If not, or if it threatens to get away from us, we fight it.

In spite of a lot of hindsight, there was no way we could have really predicted what would happen. Even knowing now how it turned out, given the same information we had back then, we would have made the same decisions we did make.

There has been a lot of discussion in some quarters that park management was at fault for not setting more prescribed fires in the park to cut down fuel loading. This ignores some basic facts about the way lodgepole pine forests function. Lodgepole pines usually only carry a fire in their crowns. By definition, a crown fire is uncontrollable. How can we set prescribed fires that will do any good and still keep them under control? Escape fires from so-called prescribed fires are common. Next time, we will come under criticism for having set the fire in the name of protecting the park from fuel buildups. Furthermore, in order to protect the park by prescribed burning, we would probably have to burn 70,000 acres a year every year from now on. The smoke alone would cast a pall over the region for hundreds of miles. By the way, one of our biggest complaints from tourists last year was about the smoke.

Recreation Group

We care about the environment and delight as much as anybody in experiencing the natural wilderness. However, there are just too many people who want to experience the wilderness to leave it in a wholly unprotected natural state. The wilderness belongs to all of us even if we live in cities far away. Yellowstone is not just for wildlife and trees. It is also for people who want to camp, hike, swim, fish, sightsee, bike, ski, and do many other activities. With proper management, there is room for all. However, wilderness regions cannot be permitted total self-regulation. They need to be maintained to serve many needs.

The primary reason these wildfires were so out of control is that we "monkeyed with the ecological system to begin with. The most important lesson that can come out of Yellowstone is how urgently we must reduce the unnatural organic fuels overload by reintroducing fire under very carefully prescribed conditions." (Russ Butcher)[11] Letting the forests burn, knowing there was so much unburned fuel lying around, was an act of negligence. We urge active control of the Yellowstone ecosystem so that plants, animals, and humans can coexist together.

Historian

The Yellowstone fires of 1988, though unprecedented in recent times, were nevertheless not unexpected. Tree-ring studies and historical record research have pointed to the fact that fires of that magnitude have occurred in the past. The relationship between the Greater Yellowstone Area and fire is long. It is a history of many small fires punctuated by big blowups.

Fire policies in Yellowstone have evolved over the more than 116 years of the park's existence. Past fire-suppression activities have contributed to the buildup of fuel leading to the 1988 conflagration. "Fire suppression was not a neutral act; it did not quick-freeze an ecosystem, which changed by having fire withheld as surely as it changed by being burned." (Stephen Pyne)[12] The change to a natural or let-burn policy in the early 1970s did not alter the fuel situation significantly. Only an area of less than 40,000 acres burned since that change—a mere fragment of the park's total area. Furthermore, the natural-burn policy ignored the historic role Native Americans played over the past several thousand years in bringing fire to Yellowstone. Indians across this country used fire to promote forage growth that would attract large food animals such as deer and elk so they could be hunted easily. They used fire in hunting to drive game out from cover and even used fire as a weapon in battles. When the park was created in 1872, it was not in pristine condition.

It is difficult to attribute blame for these fires to any one organization, because even if all the right steps to prevent them had been taken, they still might have occurred. A historian can look back at and ponder all the conditions of 1988 and examine decisions made and their consequences without the pressure of a crisis situation. In the heat of the moment, if you will excuse the expression, many life-and-death decisions have to be made. Historians, under no pressure, can look back and see if those decisions were the correct ones.

I can say that it is my belief that Yellowstone management "fell behind in national fire practices. Its once-prominent suppression organization gradually disintegrated into vestigial bits and pieces, not exactly sure of its role and shunted into other park concerns like running a helicopter. Its elaborate on-site monitoring of early fires gave way to a one-time evaluation of smoke reports, usually by aerial photos. The fire committee, which made decisions, became clubbish, haughty over its highly personalized knowledge. Yellowstone did not field a prescribed fire program: it had a let-burn program. Instead of prescription, it had a philosophy. Instead of control technologies, it had size." (Stephen Pyne)[13]

"Once the fires became large, they were a power no different from hurricanes or earthquakes over which humans have little control. But the park could have altered the fuel structure in advance of the outbreak, and it could have intervened when the fires were small." (Stephen Pyne)[14]

Administrator

I doubt if many people in this room tonight would volunteer to trade places with me. Management of a park like Yellowstone is an awesome responsibility and neither I nor any of my fellow administrators take it lightly. It is easy to look back at last year's fires and decide what we should have done. Yes, mistakes were made but the mistakes were made in good faith. We sincerely believed those decisions were in the best interests of the park's ecosystem. There were many times when we were unsure what to do but our responsibilities required us to act. Sometimes, the best act was to quell our natural instincts and stand back and let nature take its course.

It has been suggested by some that our previous policy of suppressing all fires within the park resulted in extraordinary buildups of fuel leading to the conflagration. To some very limited extent this is true. However, for most of the park, this is an exaggeration. Though the policy for a hundred years had been to suppress fires, effective fire suppression has existed for only the last thirty or forty years. The backcountry land is much too rugged for fire crews to reach in time to do any good. It is only with the innovation of using airplanes for fire fighting that fires in all parts of the park have been reachable. In other words, effective fire suppression has not had enough time to alter appreciably the fuel buildup situation. What we had, in fact, was a fuel buildup that took several hundred years to reach its peak along with unprecedented dry weather and windy conditions that could propel a fire through almost any kind of fuel.

Some speakers have criticized our natural-burn policy as some rigid rule that we stick to no matter what the conditions. This is simply untrue. The Park Service philosophy is to "allow a park that has documented the role of fire as a natural part of the ecosystem, and that has an approved fire-management plan specifying the prescriptions under which natural fires may burn, to manage each fire on an individual basis." (Walter Dabney) [15] We constantly monitored fires and weather conditions, and when it became apparent that we were seeing totally abnormal conditions, we suspended natural-burn and began all-out suppression. Before last summer's fire season ended, this region saw the largest and most expensive forest-fire suppression effort in history. Our policy is not rigid and "of course we're going to revise" it. "We just took a giant step forward in understanding fire behavior. That policy has evolved. It is not some kind of dogma we adopted in 1972." (John Varley) [16]

I would like to address one more point. Contrary to what any of you may have heard, read, or seen in the various news media, Yellowstone is not dead. "Yellowstone is still the magnificent place it always has been; fires are a part of the life processes here, and the park will heal and regenerate its natural scars as it has countless times before. I'm excited about that process. . . . We have the rare opportunity to witness wilderness regeneration on a scale rarely seen anywhere on earth. Nature is not always a gentle hostess, but she never fails to be an inspiring teacher." We are no longer looking at the old Yellowstone. It is the new Yellowstone and "it has never offered more than it does now." (Robert Barbee) [17]

Adjournment

The imaginary public meeting ended as most do with no clear answer to the stated questions. Self-interest continued to rule. At least, all sides expressed their views. Or did they? In fact, one side was left out. Unfortunately, it could not speak. It has no collective voice or even consciousness. It is the forest itself.

1. Simpson, R. W. (1988), "The Fires of '88, Yellowstone Park & Montana in Flames," *American Geographic Publishing Montana Magazine,* p. 35.
2. Ibid., p. 35.
3. Satchell, M., and Dworkin, P. (1988), "Burn baby burn! Stop baby stop!" *U.S. News & World Report,* v. 105, n. 11, p. 15.
4. Bogliano, C. (1989), "Yellowstone and the Let-Burn Policy," *American Forests,* v. 95, nos. 1 and 2, p. 24.
5. Ibid., p. 24.
6. Monastersky, R. (1988), "Lessons from the Flames," *Science News,* v. 134, n. 20, p. 317.
7. Yellowstone National Park (1989), "Yellowstone Fires 1988," p. 2.
8. Bogliano, C. (1989), "Yellowstone and the Let-Burn Policy," *American Forests,* v. 95, nos. 1 and 2, p. 24.
9. Ibid., p. 24.
10. Monastersky, R. (1988), "After the Flames—Awaiting the Regeneration of Yellowstone," *Science News,* v. 134, n. 21, p. 330.
11. Milstein, M. (1988), "The Long, Hot Summer," *National Parks,* v. 62, nos. 11 and 12, p. 50.
12. Pyne, S. J. (1989), "The Summer We Let Wild Fire Loose," *Natural History Magazine,* v. 98, no. 8, p. 46.
13. Ibid., p. 47.
14. Ibid., p. 47.
15. Bogliano, C. (1989), "Yellowstone and the Let-Burn Policy," *American Forests,* v. 95, nos. 1 and 2, p. 23.
16. Monastersky, R (1988), "Lessons from the Flames," *Science News,* v. 134, n. 20, p. 316.
17. Yellowstone National Park (1989), "Yellowstone Fires 1988," p. 1.

EPILOGUE:
TRAVELS THROUGH
YELLOWSTONE

TRAVELS THROUGH YELLOWSTONE

As the five-day visit my daughter Allison and I made to Yellowstone came to an end, I was amazed at how quickly my mood of foreboding had changed to one of excitement and discovery. I guess two moose had a lot to do with it. Just minutes after Allison and I passed the ranger station, at the park's East Gate, early in the evening on our first night there, we saw a bull moose, with its just-sprouting rack of antlers, browsing casually along the roadside. I had been ready for the worst—mile upon blackened mile of desolate landscape. Instead, there was a moose seemingly unperturbed by our presence, stuffing itself on the green vegetation at the roadside. Moments later, we spotted a second moose lying in the grass in the midst of a clearing surrounded by healthy green trees. The moose was lazily munching on grass and again seemed not to be bothered by anything—even our presence. Perhaps these moose had been affected by last year's fires but there was no sign of fire scars anywhere. It was business as usual. It was not something I had expected.

A light snow began to fall as we drove higher up to the snowy Sylvan Pass, where plows had recently cleared the roadway of six-foot drifts, and over and down into the great plateau. Fire obviously hadn't reached here, but where had it reached? It was many miles before we saw our first fire sign, a new clearing with only stubbly charred snags and ash-covered soil. We were to learn that much of the park was abundantly green and it was hard to look in any direction without seeing elk or bison or the little creatures like chipmunks, marmots, or birds. The park was alive and vital, yet there were also the burned areas of black snags protruding upward from ashy gray soil as though in defiance of the fires.

Last year's television pictures of nature gone crazy were quickly replaced in my mind by a more balanced and less sensational view. The fires had not swept the park clean. Instead, the park existed as a mosaic or patchwork quilt of green, brown, and black. Large mountainsides, like those in the Mammoth Hot Springs area, had city-block-size black scars where the fire had raged. But these irregular-shaped patches of black, which followed ridge lines, were surrounded by a ring of brown—trees that were heat damaged and killed but not burned by the fires. The dry, brown needles still clung to the lodgepole branches. Surrounding them were green trees still in the fullness of growth. For those trees, it was as though the fire had never existed.

The pattern was the same throughout the park—black, brown, green. On some trees, the fire seemed so focused that all three colors were present. It was obvious that the fire had not moved through the whole park like some juggernaut, but instead skipped its way through, blackening some acres and leaving others alone. At first glance, the meadows and marshes seemed totally bypassed by the fires. One morning, in the lush, willowy marshes located in the middle of the perimeter of the infamous North Fork Fire, we saw a group of seven moose and nearby was a small herd of elk. All were grazing. Surely fire hadn't come through here, but it had. We soon began to recognize fire signs. There were blackened patches of soil where sagebrush once grew. Surface fire had moved through, but the roots of grass and shrubby plants had survived and recovered in the spring with abundant foliage.

Many times, we stopped to walk through the burned lodgepole pines. It was not some eerie moonscape. Trees were dead but most were standing. Those that were downed and heaped upon each other looked as though some giant had used them for a game of Pick-Up Stix. I was surprised at the absence of a burned odor. The winter snows had cleansed the forest and I was struck with a sense of peace and calmness. The sound of a woodpecker carried on the light breeze. The fire's heat had sculpted the tree snags and I mused that if an artist had shaped these trees, they would have brought a good price at an art gallery. A few trees even looked like fish backbones, with short branches resembling ribs. Kicking the soil sent up a small ash cloud, but beneath was healthy soil and living roots. Sprouting all about me were yellow wildflowers of a kind I did not recognize, and brilliant green patches of grass. It was the same story in every burned area we examined.

Were the fires of 1988 good or bad for the Greater Yellowstone Area? As grim and as stark as some of the burned areas were, I had no sense that the forest had ended. All about me were signs that it had only changed. Perhaps my ability to answer my question was being hampered by my narrow and limited view. I was examining a five-day slice of the Yellowstone ecosystem—an ecosystem that is thousands of years old. My view was much too limited. I was looking at the forests and meadows through human eyes and filtering what I saw through human needs and human emotions. If the forest had eyes, what would it see? If it could testify at human hearings, what would it say? It might see the fires of 1988 as a momentary blemish, a restructuring, a redistribution, and a rejuvenation. It might say, "I have been through this before and will again."

Yellowstone was born of fire. The geysers and hot

springs, for which it is famous, are signs of the great thermal activity still going on within the Earth miles beneath the surface. The Yellowstone forests and meadows were there long before we came to them. They were old before the pyramids of Egypt were built. And they will be there long after we are gone. We left the park certain that Yellowstone will absorb the fires. Some areas will recover slowly while others have already burst into green. I personally have come to know that human charges and countercharges and blame-casting means nothing to the forest. Perhaps, if any fault exists in regard to the 1988 fires, it exists within each of us for expecting nature to do what we want it to and do so at our convenience.

Forest Fire Fighters

Forest fire fighters are all kinds of people. Many are professional fire fighters while others are part-time fire fighters who are college students, park naturalists, or have other careers during the low-fire-danger seasons. Fire fighters are employed by state natural resources agencies, national forests, the Bureau of Land Management, and the National Park Service. If you are interested in a career in forest fire fighting, contact any of the following agencies for more information:

State Departments of Natural Resources
National Forests Offices (check state maps to find which forests are found in the regions you are interested in working in)
Bureau of Land Management District Offices
National Park Service

GLOSSARY

Aerial bombers—Airplanes designed to carry water and fire-retardant mixtures to forest fires for bombing drops on the fire head.

Backburn—A fire-fighting technique where fire fighters deliberately set fire to unburned forests, hoping the inward blowing wind, caused by the advancing wild-fire, will draw the new flames toward itself to create a wide fire line of already-burned fuels.

BTU—British thermal unit. A measure of the heat given off by burning materials.

Conduction—Heat transfer by direct contact.

Control line—A combination of natural barriers and fire lines constructed by fire fighters to stop the advance of a fire.

Convection—Heat transfer by the physical movement of heated particles such as gas molecules.

Crown fire—A dangerous fire that advances rapidly through the tops (crowns) of trees.

Fire—A violent chemical reaction in which carbon or other compounds quickly combine with oxygen to release flames, smoke, heat, and waste gases.

Fire behavior—The manner in which a fire develops.

Fire ecology—The study of the relationships of plants, animals, and the nonliving environment to fire.

Fire head—The advancing flame front of a fire.

Fire interval—The length of time between fires.

Fire line—A wide path across the advance of a fire that is cleared of fuels by fire fighters.

Fire spread—The way fires move through various fuels.

Fire storm—A major crown fire driven by high winds, sometimes of hurricane force.

Fire triangle—The three things needed for fire: heat, oxygen, and fuel.

Flame development—The shape of the flames.

Ground fire—A fire that creeps through forest duff of pine needles and leaf litter.

Heat value—The heat released by various fuels.

Helispot—A small clearing constructed in a forest to permit helicopters to land.

Helitack—Fire fighter teams and equipment that are deployed by helicopters.

Hotshot—A crew of highly trained fire fighters assigned to dig fire lines and control fires.

Let-burn—A policy, better described as "natural burn," that permits certain fires to burn naturally.

McLeod—A fire-fighting tool that combines a rake with a hoe.

Natural burn—A policy, also called "let-burn," that permits certain fires to burn naturally.

Orographic effect—An upwelling produced when air masses move over land of higher elevation.

Osbourn fire finder—A sighting tool for accurate position location of fires.

Prescribed fire—A fire that is deliberately set to burn out fuel accumulations, thereby preventing huge wildfires from forming.

Pulaski—A fire-fighting tool that combines an ax with a hoe.

Radiation—Heat transfer through radiant energy.

Salvo—A water-bomber technique where the entire load of water or fire retardants are dropped at one time.

Smoke chaser—A small crew that is assigned to reach small fires before they have a chance to blow up.

Smoke jumper—Fire fighters who parachute from cargo planes to fight remote fires.

Surface fire—A fire that moves through downed branches, shrubs, and grasses.

Trail drop—A sequential drop of water or fire retardant by a water bomber to create a long, narrow, wetted-down trail across the advance of a fire.

Wildfire—An uncontrolled fire.

SOURCES

Bogliano, C. (1989), "Yellowstone and the Let-Burn Policy," *American Forests,* v. 95, nos. 1 and 2.

Carrier, J. (1989), *Summer of Fire: The Great Yellowstone Fires of 1988,* Salt Lake City: Peregrine Smith Books.

Chandler, C., et al. (1983), *Fire in Forestry,* vols. 1 and 2, New York: John Wiley & Sons.

Cone, P. (1989), "Yellowstone's Bombers: Fighting the Firestorm," *Flying,* v. 116, n. 1.

de Golia, J. (1989), *Fire—The Story Behind a Force of Nature,* Las Vegas, NV: KC Publications, Inc.

Linkewich, A. (1972), *Air Attack on Forest Fires, History and Techniques,* Calgary, Alberta: D. W. Friesen and Sons, Ltd.

Loeffelbein, B. (May 1984), "Smokey Hits 401!," *American Forests,* v. 90.

Milstein, M. (1988), *"The Long, Hot Summer: Rare Conditions Spark An Inferno at Yellowstone and Test Public Policy," National Parks,* v. 62, nos. 11 and 12.

Monastersky, R. (1988), "After the Flames—Awaiting the Regeneration of Yellowstone," *Science News,* v. 134, n. 21.

Monastersky, R. (1988), "Lessons from the Flames," *Science News,* v. 134, n. 20.

Morgan, C. (April 1988), "Wildfire!", *Reader's Digest,* v. 132.

National Park Service and U.S. Forest Service (1989), *The Greater Yellowstone Postfire Assessment.*

National Park Service (1989), *Yellowstone Fires 1988,* (supplement to the *Yellowstone Today* newspaper).

National Park Service, *The Greater Yellowstone Fires of 1988—Questions and Answers.* (News media fact sheet provided by the park management at Yellowstone National Park.)

National Wildfire Coordinating Group (1986), *Firefighters Guide,* Boise Interagency Fire Center, section 43.1.

Nieman, S. (1985), "Wired Forests," *American Forests,* v. 91, n. 6.

Perry, D. G. (1987), *Wildland Firefighting—Fire Behavior, Tactics & Command* Bellflower, CA: Fire Publications, Inc.

Pyne, S. J. (1982), *Fire in America: A Cultural History of Wildland and Rural Fire,* Princeton, NJ: Princeton University Press.

Pyne, S. J. (1984), *Introduction to Wildland Fire—Fire Management in the United States,* New York: John Wiley & Sons.

Pyne, S. J. (August 1989), "The Summer We Let Wild Fire Loose," *Natural History Magazine,* v. 98.

Randall, C. E. (1969), "Crazy Blazes," *American Forests,* v. 75, n. 8.

Robinson, C. D. (1872), "Account of the Great Peshtigo Fire of 1871," report on forestry submitted to Congress by the Commissioner of Agriculture, Washington, D.C.: Government Printing Office.

Satchell, M., and Dworkin, P. (1988), "Burn Baby Burn! Stop Baby Stop!", *U.S. News & World Report,* v. 105, n. 11.

Schullery, P. (1989), "Yellowstone's Fire Regime," paper supplied by the National Park Service.

Simpson, R. W. (1988), "The Fires of '88, Yellowstone Park & Montana in Flames," *American Geographic Publishing, Montana Magazine.*

Staff Writer (1989), "Turbine Engines Will Improve CL-

215's Firefighting Capability," *Aviation and Space Technology,* v. 131, n. 8.

Turbak, G. (September 1986), "To Hell and Back in a Pup Tent," *American Forests,* v. 92.

USDA (1986), "Your Fire Shelter," Forest Service Equipment Center.

Utley, R. M. (1982), "National Parks," *American History Illustrated,* v. 17, n. 1.

Witkin, G. (June 1986), Fighting Forest Fires the High-tech Way, *U.S. News & World Report,* v. 100.

Wright, H. A., and Bailey, A. W. (1982), *Fire Ecology—United States and Southern Canada,* New York: John Wiley & Sons.

Wuerthner, G. (1988), *Yellowstone and the Fires of Change,* Salt Lake City: Haggis House Publications, Inc.

Yellowstone National Park (1989), "Yellowstone Fires 1988."

FOR FURTHER READING

de Golia, J. (1989), *Fire—The Story Behind a Force of Nature*. Las Vegas, NV: KC Publications, Inc. (Interesting account of fire fighting and research.)

Carrier, J. (1989), *Summer of Fire: The Great Yellowstone Fires of 1988*. Salt Lake City: Peregrine Smith Books. (An excellent account of the Yellowstone fires.)

Linkewich, A. (1972), *Air Attack on Forest Fires, History and Techniques*. Calgary, Alberta: D. W. Friesen and Sons, Ltd. (Somewhat dated but very interesting.)

Perry, D. G. (1987), *Wildland Firefighting—Fire Behavior, Tactics & Command*. Bellflower, CA: Fire Publications, Inc. (Detailed description of fire-fighting organization and tactics.)

Pyne, S. (1984), *Introduction to Wildland Fire—Fire Management in the United States*. New York: John Wiley & Sons, Inc. (Somewhat difficult but a good source on fire-fighting methods.)

Pyne, S. J. (1982), *Fire in America: A Cultural History of Wildland and Rural Fire*. Princeton, NJ: Princeton University Press. (Difficult, but a good account of the history of forest fire fighting in America.)

Simpson, R. W. (1988), "The Fires of '88, Yellowstone Park & Montana in Flames." *American Geographic Publishing Montana Magazine*. (Interesting account of the 1988 Yellowstone fires.)

Wright, H. A., and Bailey, A. W. (1982), *Fire Ecology—United States and Southern Canada*. New York:

John Wiley & Sons. (A classic book on the role of fire in nature. Difficult.)

Wuerthner, G. (1988), *Yellowstone and the Fires of Change*. Salt Lake City: Haggis House Publications, Inc. (An excellent account of the Yellowstone fires and fire ecology.)

INDEX

ABOUT THE AUTHOR

Gregory Vogt has written a number of books on scientific topics for Franklin Watts, including *Electricity and Magnetism, A Twenty-Fifth Anniversary Album of NASA, Space Laboratories,* and *Predicting Volcanic Eruptions.* He lives in Oklahoma with his wife and three daughters.

DATE DUE

FOLLETT